# BLUES GUITAR

Approved Curriculum

## The Complete Acoustic Blues Guitar Method

**Beginning • Intermediate • Mastering**

**LOU MANZI**

Alfred, the leader in educational publishing, and the National Guitar Workshop, one of America's finest guitar schools, have joined forces to bring you the best, most progressive educational tools possible. We hope you will enjoy this book and encourage you to look for other fine products from Alfred and the National Guitar Workshop.

ISBN 0-7390-3673-4 (Book & CD)

*This book was acquired, edited and produced by Workshop Arts, Inc., the publishing arm of the National Guitar Workshop.*
*Nathaniel Gunod, managing and acquisitions editor*
*Burgess Speed, editor*
*Ante Gelo, music typesetter*
*Timothy Phelps, interior design and photography*
*CD recorded by Colin Tilton at Bar None Studio, Northford, CT.*
*The guitar used on the CD and in all photos of the author was made by Thomas Bazzolo (www.bazzolo.com).*

*Cover photograph © David Redfern / Redferns*

# TABLE OF CONTENTS

# ABOUT THE AUTHOR

PHOTO BY TIMOTHY PHELPS • COURTESY OF WORKSHOP ARTS PUBLICATIONS

Lou Manzi has been performing his original and dynamic style of acoustic blues since the 1970s. He has written four fingerstyle guitar books, including *Beginning Fingerstyle Guitar* (The National Guitar Workshop/Alfred #14099). Lou has performed extensively as a solo artist and with Rob Fletcher as half of the Fletcher & Manzi duo. Their CD, *Horsin' Around Live,* features original songs that are a blend of blues, jazz and rock. He also appears on *Remembrance*, a compilation CD that is a tribute to American veterans.

Lou is a guitar instructor at several Connecticut schools and has taught at the National Guitar Workshop since 1984. Recognized as a prominent teacher of the acoustic guitar and the blues, he has conducted seminars throughout the United States.

## DEDICATION

*Beginning Acoustic Blues Guitar* is dedicated to my parents. I saw the Beatles. I wanted a guitar. They bought one for me. One gift among millions of others.

## ACKNOWLEDGEMENTS

Thanks to Ronnie Earl whose music showed me how strong and deep the blues can be; to Nat and the staffs of Workshop Arts and Alfred for the opportunity to share with others my love of the music; to Dave, Barbara, Paula and all my friends at the National Guitar Workshop, for all they've given me over the years; and to Rob Fletcher for all the fun and inspiration.

# ABOUT THIS BOOK

You've made a great choice in learning to play the blues—and what better instrument to play them on than the acoustic guitar, which has been a beloved sidekick to blues players since the earliest days of the style. If you're a true beginner, you'll find the first steps in this book easy and fun. There is also a lot to offer the more experienced player. Either way, you're sure to find the blues a rich and rewarding style to play.

With a little practice, most of the musical examples in this book will be easy to master. The music on the CD will probably sound familiar to you; many great blues artists use the techniques in this book. Make it your goal to learn all of the music in each chapter and you'll be well on your way to becoming a real blues player.

You don't have to go through the book page by page. You may find it more fun to jump around. Play the easier examples first and, as you improve, begin to work on more difficult material. Another option is to listen to the CD and tackle your favorite examples or songs first. Make sure, however, to learn the music theory that is covered; it will make you a better player.

The blues has deeply influenced rock, jazz, country, R&B and almost every other style of music. As a blues player, you will be familiar with many elements found in these other styles and have a good head start when learning any contemporary music.

The blues is like a well. You can scoop some water from the surface and get a refreshing drink. This would be like a person taking their first steps, learning a few songs. But the well is *deep,* and there's *good* water all the way to the bottom. You can play the blues for years and continue to learn and drink from this well. Your mastery of the material in this book is just your first drink. Enjoy!

00

Track 1

A compact disc is available with this book. Using the disc will help make learning more enjoyable and the information more meaningful. Listening to the CD will help you correctly interpret the rhythms and feel of each example. The symbol on the left appears next to each song or example that is performed on the CD. Example numbers are above the symbol. The track number below each symbol corresponds directly to the song or example you want to hear. Track 1 will help you tune to this CD.

# CHAPTER 1

# Getting Started

## CHOOSING STRINGS

Walk into any well stocked music store and you will see the inevitable "Wall of Strings." Choosing a set of strings for your guitar can be confusing for a beginner.

How often you need to change your strings depends on how much you play and your personal taste. Newer strings will always sound brighter than older ones. Older strings lose their tone, do not stay in tune as well and may even start to rust. Don't let your strings get to that point. You should change them when they start to lose their brilliance.

To play acoustically, you need *acoustic guitar strings*. The 3rd, 4th, 5th and 6th strings are thin steel cores wound in thin bronze.

Strings come in different thicknesses or *gauges*. Most of the sets you'll see in stores are *extra light*, *light* and *medium* gauge. Try different gauges now and then to see which you prefer for your guitar. As a rule, the thicker the string, the richer the tone. However, there is a disadvantage to using thicker strings. They are more difficult to play. The thicker the string, the more effort is needed to press the strings against the frets. Keep in mind that certain chords are much easier to play with thinner strings. Another reason to use light gauge strings is that you'll be learning how to *bend* strings. This requires you to push or pull a string either up or down. This is easier to accomplish with lighter strings.

You can also use *custom light* gauge strings, which are somewhere between light and extra light. The sound is good and they are easy to play, which is very important if you play a lot. It is important to keep your hands in good health.

## THE OPEN STRINGS

The thinnest string, the one closest to the floor, is the *1st string*. The others are numbered consecutively to the thickest string, the *6th string*, which is closest to the ceiling. It will be helpful to memorize the names of the strings (included in the chart below) as soon as possible. The sentence, "**E**rnie's **A**nt **D**oes **G**et **B**ig **E**ventually," can help you in this process.

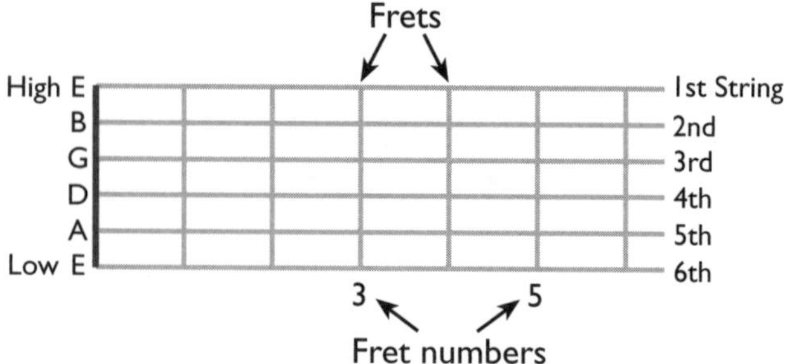

# TUNING

You can tune by matching your strings to the tuning notes on Track 1 of the CD for this book. Here are two other ways you can tune your guitar.

## ELECTRONIC TUNER

The best way for a beginner to tune is to use an *electronic tuner.* Not only is this the quickest, easiest and most reliable way, it also accustoms the beginner's musical "ear" to how the strings are supposed to sound. Most professional players use electronic tuners because of their speed and accuracy—and because they allow performers to tune quietly (which is very useful during a performance).

There are two types of tuners: *guitar tuners* and *chromatic tuners.* A guitar tuner is designed to tune the strings in *standard tuning:* E–A–D–G–B–E. A chromatic tuner allows you to tune a string to any *pitch* (degree of highness or lowness of a *tone* or musical sound). This is helpful when using *alternate tunings,* which are any tunings *other* than standard tuning.

## RELATIVE TUNING

It is also vitally important that you learn to tune without an electronic tuner. You can do this using *relative tuning*, where the strings are tuned by comparing their pitches to one another.

To use this method, you need a *reference tone.* You can get this from a tuning fork, a pitch pipe, a piano or another guitar. A good pitch to start with is E (12 white keys below middle C on the piano), to which you would match your 6th string. If you do not have a reference pitch to start with, approximate it the best you can. As long as all the strings are tuned in relation to each other, your guitar will sound in tune.

1. Match the open 6th string (low E—the string closest to your chin when the guitar is placed in proper playing position, see page 17) to your reference tone (E).
2. Match the open 5th string to the A on the 5th fret of the 6th string.
3. Match the open 4th string to the D on the 5th fret of the 5th string.
4. Match the open 3rd string to the G on the 5th fret of the 4th string.
5. Match the open 2nd string to the B on the 4th fret of the 3rd string.
6. Match the open 1st string to the E on the 5th fret of the 2nd string.

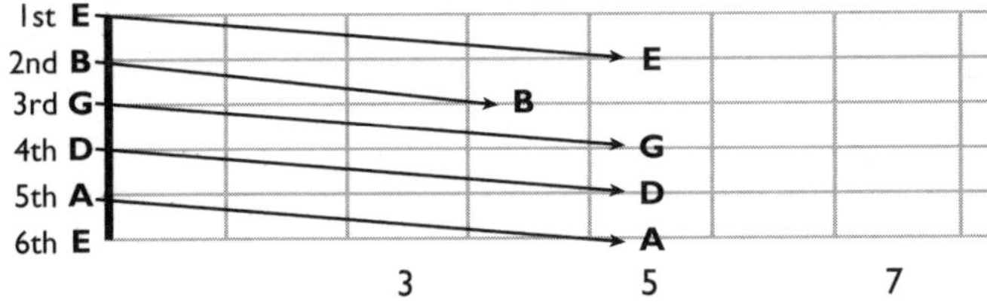

You can also tune to Track 1 of the CD.

# MUSICAL PITCHES AND THE FRETBOARD

## HALF STEPS AND WHOLE STEPS

A *half step* is the distance of one fret on the guitar. For example, press any string at any fret. Now go one fret higher (closer to the body of the guitar). The distance between those two pitches is a half step.

A *whole step* is the distance of two frets on the guitar, or two half steps. Once again, press any string at any fret. Now go two frets higher (skip one fret). The distance between those two pitches is a whole step.

From any open string to the 1st fret is the distance of a half step. From any open string to the 2nd fret is a whole step.

## THE MUSICAL ALPHABET

The *musical alphabet* consists of seven letters that repeat: A–B–C–D–E–F–G, A–B–C, etc. Each of these letters represents a musical pitch. These seven pitches are the *natural* pitches. On a piano, they are the white keys.

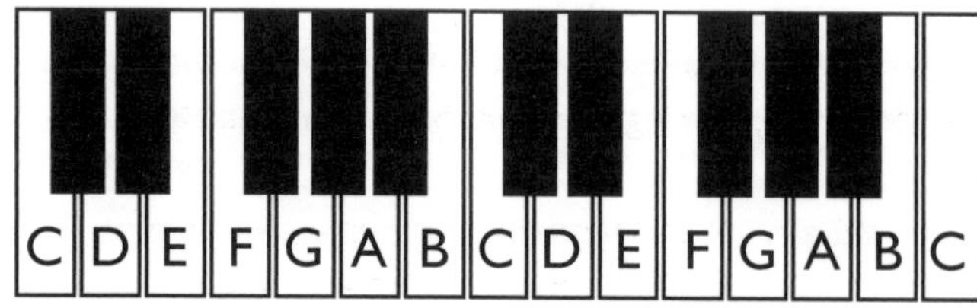


Only two sets of natural pitches are a half step apart: E–F and B–C.

## ACCIDENTALS

The pitches between the natural pitches are *accidentals.* The symbols used to represent them are:

♯ *Sharp.* Raises a pitch one half step (one fret).

♭ *Flat.* Lowers a pitch one half step (one fret).

♮ *Natural.* Returns a pitch to its natural position.

These raised and lowered pitches are the black keys on a piano.

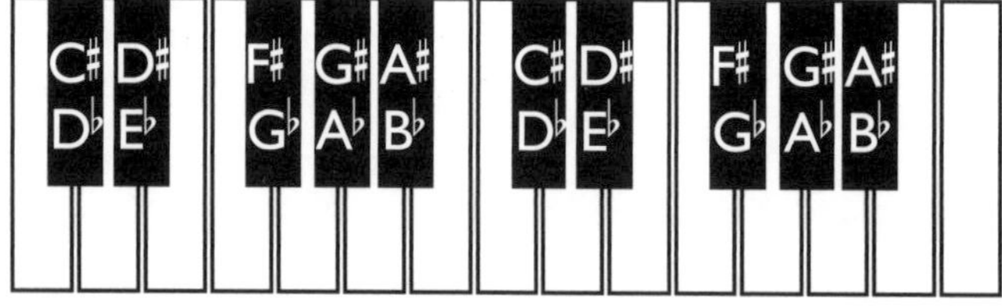


Notice that each black key, or pitch between the natural pitches, has two names. Each of these can be viewed as a raised tone (when moving a half step up from a white key) or a lowered tone (when moving a half step down from a white key). Because of this, they can be called by a sharp name or a flat name (depending on the musical situation). For example, the first black key in the illustration above can be called C♯ or D♭. The two names given to the same pitch are called *enharmonic equivalents.*

When combined, the natural pitches and accidentals make up the 12 pitches used to play music. Notice that the letters repeat themselves in the illustration below. This is because the pitch-names repeat every 12 half steps. The distance of 12 half steps between two pitches with the same name is an *octave*. Because an instrument usually spans several octaves, there are many more tone choices than the 12 actual pitch-names.

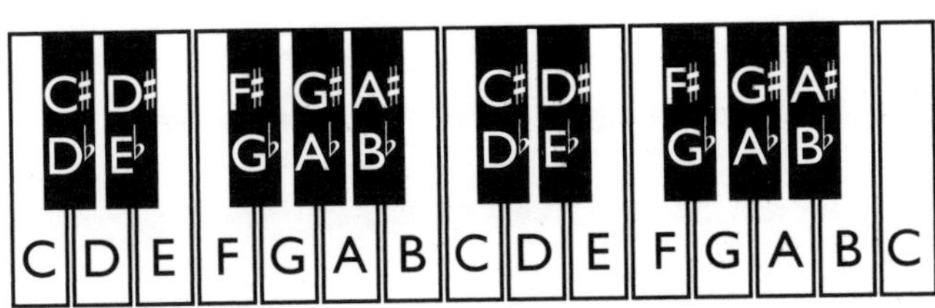


## THE GUITAR FRETBOARD

On the guitar we don't have the visual aid of black and white keys; all the frets look the same. However, the same chromatic (half-step) principle makes it easy for us to name every note on the guitar. The following chart gives the names of the pitches on each string—from the open strings to the 17th fret.

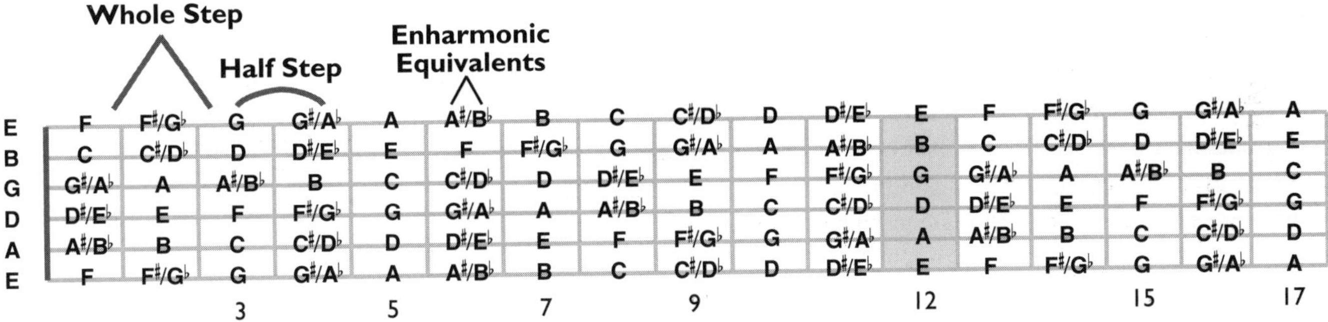


If you start with any open string and go 12 half steps (12 frets) up (toward the body), you will have gone the distance of an octave and played every pitch-name there is. Notice also, you will have arrived at the letter with which you started. E is the open 1st string; if you go to the 12th fret, you arrive again at E. This is the same for all the strings and for every pitch.

### Learn the fretboard

1. Start by memorizing the string names (if you haven't already).
2. Then apply the musical alphabet, keeping in mind the two sets of natural pitches that are a half step apart (E–F, B–C).
3. Go string by string. First, name all the natural pitches. Then, using accidentals, name ALL the pitches.

Learning the fretboard is essential for a guitarist. Not only will it prove useful throughout this book, but also throughout your experience as a guitar player.

# STANDARD MUSIC NOTATION

To get the most out of this book (and future studies), a functional knowledge of *standard music notation* is necessary. Even the great Howlin' Wolf took classes to learn this way of writing and reading music.

## PITCH

Pitch is the aspect of standard music notation that indicates the degree of highness or lowness of a musical tone.

### Notes

Music is written by placing *notes* on a *staff*. Notes appear in various ways.

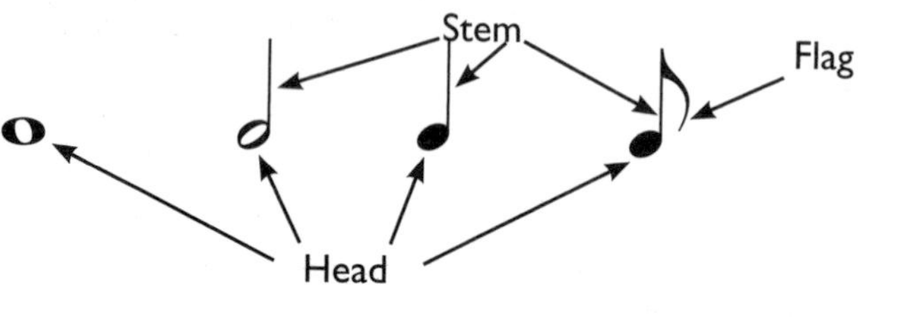


### The Staff and Clef

The staff has five lines and four spaces which are read from left to right. At the beginning of the staff is a *clef*. The clef dictates what notes correspond to a particular line or space on the staff. Guitar music is written in *treble clef* 𝄞 which is sometimes called the *G clef*. The ending curl of the clef circles the G line on the staff.

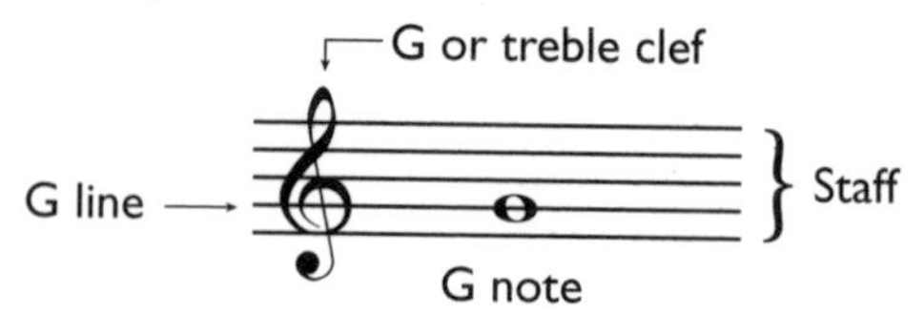


Here are the notes on the staff using the G clef.

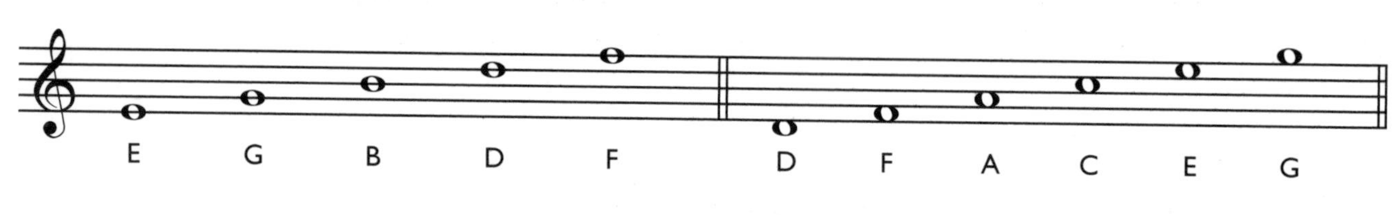


### Ledger Lines

The higher a note appears on the staff, the higher it sounds. When a note is too high or too low to be written on the staff, *ledger lines* are used.

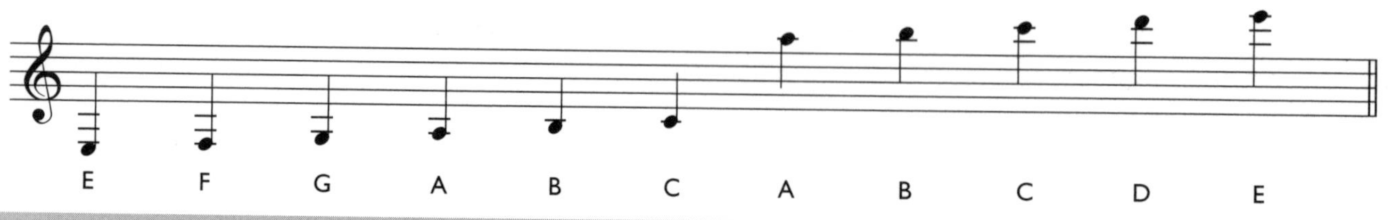


For reasons of convenience and easy reading, guitar music is written one octave higher than it sounds.

## TIME

Musical time is measured in *beats*. Beats are the steady pulse of the music on which we build *rhythms*. Rhythm is a pattern of long and short sounds and silences and is represented by *note* and *rest values*. Value indicates duration.

### Measures and Bar Lines

The staff is divided by vertical lines called *bar lines*. The space between two bar lines is a *measure* or *bar*. Measures divide music into groups of beats. A *double bar* marks the end of a section or example.

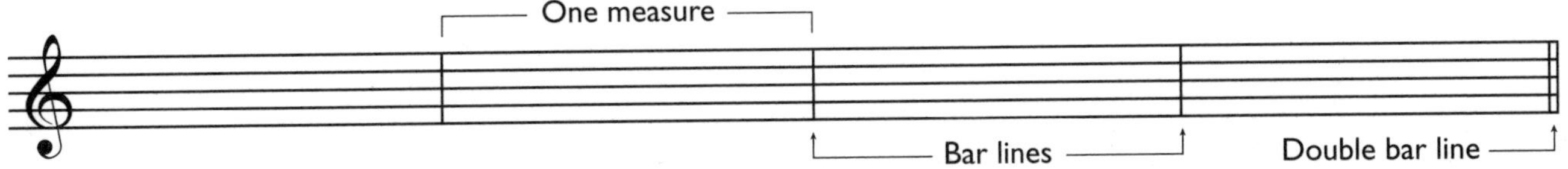


### Note Values

The duration of a note—its value—is indicated by the note's appearance or shape.

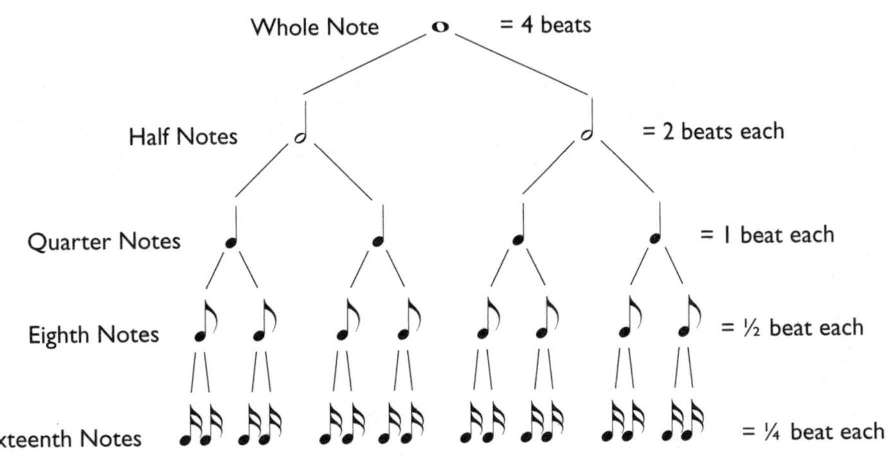


### Time Signatures

A *time signature* appears at the beginning of a piece of music. The number on top indicates the number of beats per measure. The number on the bottom indicates the type of note that gets one beat.

4/4 = 4 beats per measure
Quarter note ♩ = one beat

3/4 = 3 beats per measure
Quarter note ♩ = one beat

6/8 = 6 beats per measure
Eighth note ♪ = one beat

Sometimes a **C** is used in place of 4/4.
This is called *common time*.

**Rest Values**

Every note value has a corresponding *rest* value. A rest indicates silence in music. A *whole rest* indicates four beats of silence, a *half rest* is two beats of silence, etc.

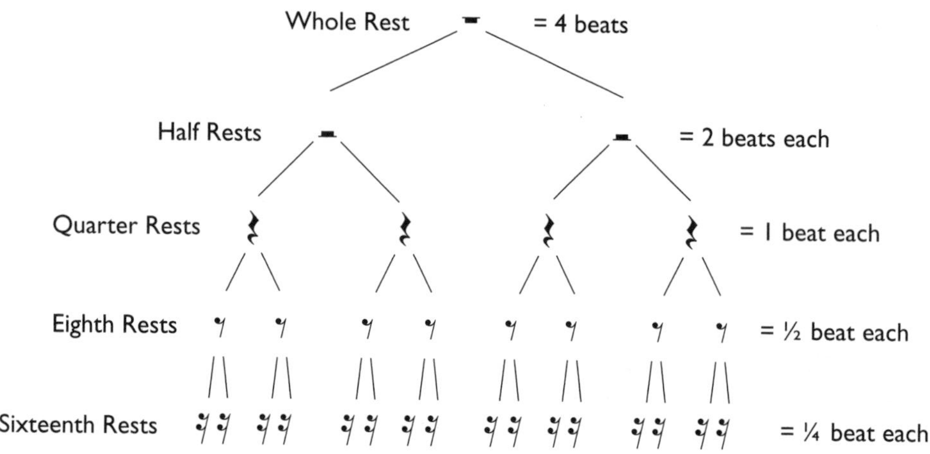


**Beaming**

Notes that are less than one beat in duration are often *beamed* together. Sometimes they are grouped in twos and sometimes they are grouped in fours.

**Ties and Counting**

A *tie* is a curved line that joins two or more notes of the same pitch that last the duration of the combined note values. For example, when a half note (two beats) is tied to a quarter note (one beat), the combined notes are held for three beats (2 + 1 = 3).

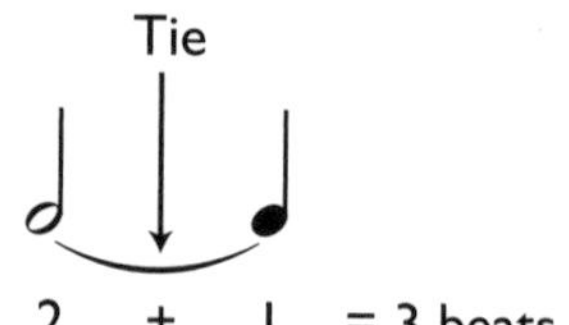


Notice the numbers under the staff in the examples below. These indicate how to count while playing. Both of these examples are in $\frac{4}{4}$ time, so we count four beats in each measure. *Eighth-note* rhythms are counted "1–&, 2–&, 3–&," etc. The numbers are the *onbeats* and the "&"s (pronounced "and") are the *offbeats*.

## Dots

A *dot* increases the length of a note or rest by one half of its original value. For instance, a half note lasts for two beats. Half of its value is one beat (a quarter note). So a *dotted half note* equals three beats (2 + 1 = 3), which is the same as a half note tied to a quarter note. The same logic applies for all dotted notes.

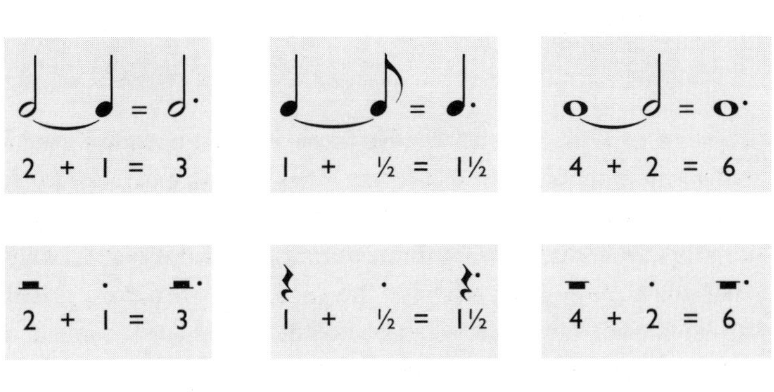


Dotted notes are especially important when the time signature is $\frac{3}{4}$, because the longest note value that will fit in a measure is a dotted half note. Also, dotted notes are very important in $\frac{6}{8}$ time, because not only is a dotted half note the longest possible note value, but a dotted quarter note is exactly half of a measure (counted: 1–&–ah, 2–&–ah).

## Triplets

A *triplet* is three notes in the time of two, or a group of three notes that, together, make up one unit of musical time, such as a beat.

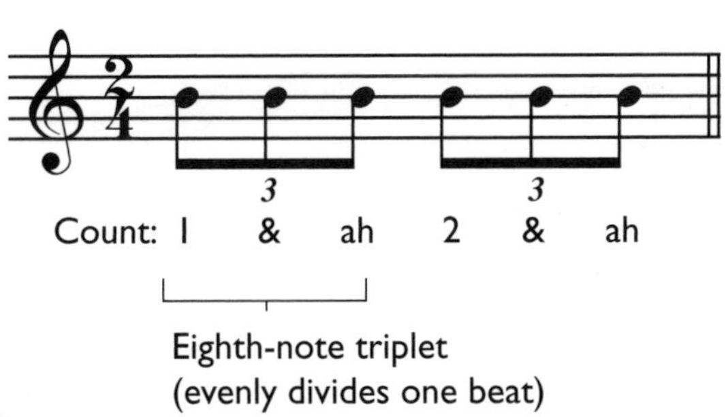


Eighth-note triplet
(evenly divides one beat)

## Repeat Signs

*Repeat signs* are used to indicate music that should be repeated.

Go back to the beginning and play these measures one more time.

Play the music between these signs twice.

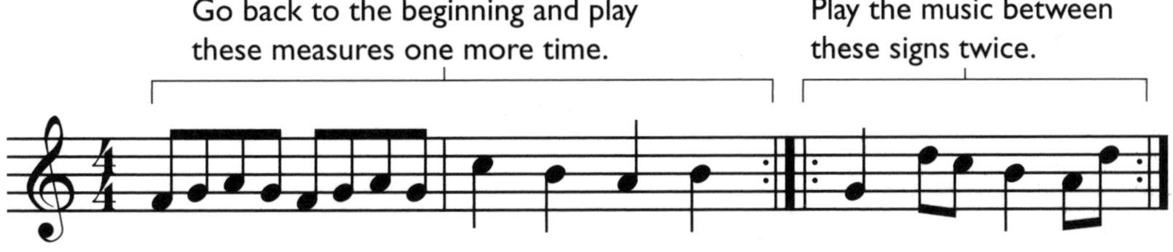

This sign 𝄎 tells us to repeat the previous measure.

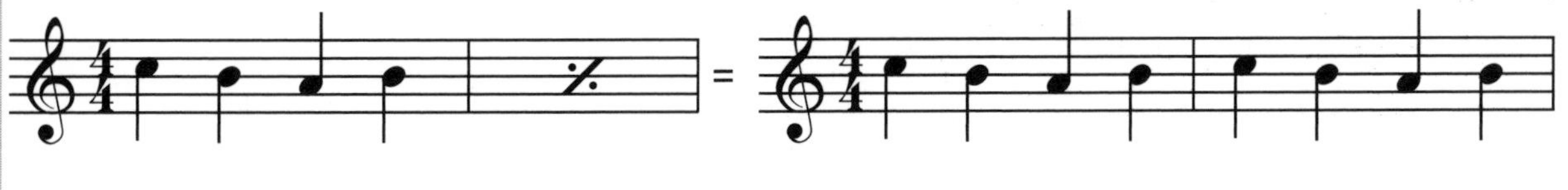

# READING TABLATURE

*Tablature,* or TAB, is an alternative form of music notation used for guitar and other fretted string instruments. In various forms, it has been in existence for hundreds of years. Tablature tells you the location, on the fretboard, of each note to be played. It provides string and fret numbers, whereas standard music notation provides pitches only—it is the guitarist's choice where to play any given pitch (on the guitar there are many places where any particular pitch can be played). Tablature, when combined with standard music notation, provides the most complete system for communicating the many possibilities in guitar playing.

Rhythm is not indicated in TAB; for that, you must refer to the standard music notation.

Six lines are used to indicate the six strings of the guitar. The top line is the high-E string and the bottom line is the low-E string.

Numbers are placed on these lines to indicate frets. If there is a "0," play that string open. The fingers of the left hand are numbered 1–4, starting with the index finger. Left-hand fingerings are indicated underneath the TAB staff.

In the following example, the first note is played with the 1st finger on the 1st fret of the 1st string. The next note is played with the 2nd finger on the 2nd fret of the 1st string. The next note is the open 1st string and the last note is played with the 4th finger on the 4th fret of the 1st string.

*Left-hand finger numbers.*

In TAB, a tied note is written in parentheses.

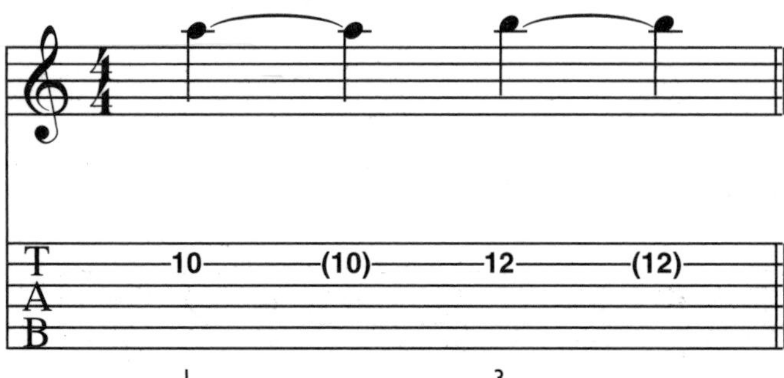

# READING SCALE AND CHORD DIAGRAMS

## SCALE DIAGRAMS

A *scale* is an arrangement of pitches in a particular order of whole steps and half steps. A *scale diagram* illustrates the pitches of a scale that are to be played one at a time, in succession.

Scale diagrams are oriented horizontally. The horizontal lines represent the strings. The vertical lines represent the frets. Dots tell us where to place our fingers on the fretboard.

Scale diagrams are read bottom-to-top, left-to-right. For example, in the diagram below, we would start with 6th string, 5th fret. Then we would go to the 6th string, 8th fret. Then to the 5th string, 5th fret—5th string, 7th fret—4th string, 5th fret—and then end on the 4th string, 7th fret.

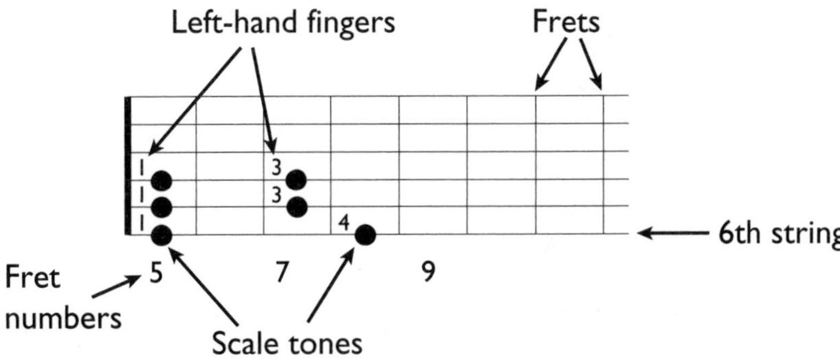


## CHORD DIAGRAMS

A *chord* is three or more tones played simultaneously. A *chord diagram* shows how it is to be played. Chord diagrams are oriented vertically. The vertical lines represent the strings. The horizontal lines represent frets.

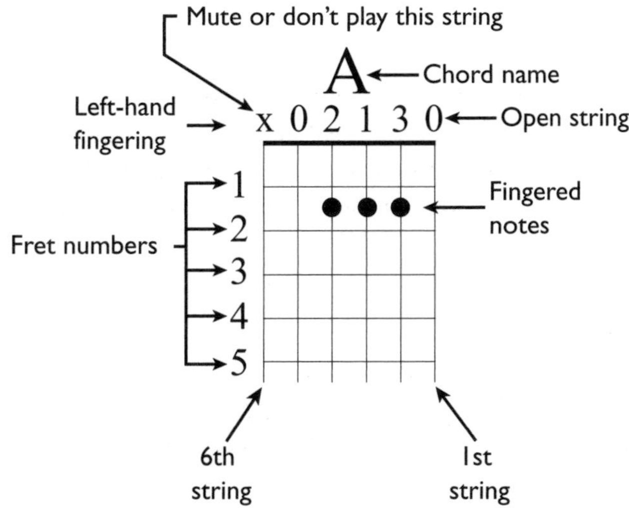

# READING CHORD CHARTS

A *chord chart* is a way of writing the *chord progression* (series of chords) for a song or piece of music. It does not give the *melody* or tune of the composition, just the chord changes. The chords are written above the staff. Sometimes, the strum or rhythm is written on the staff below the chord names in *slash notation* (which does not specify rhythm).

**Chord Chart (Slash Notation)**

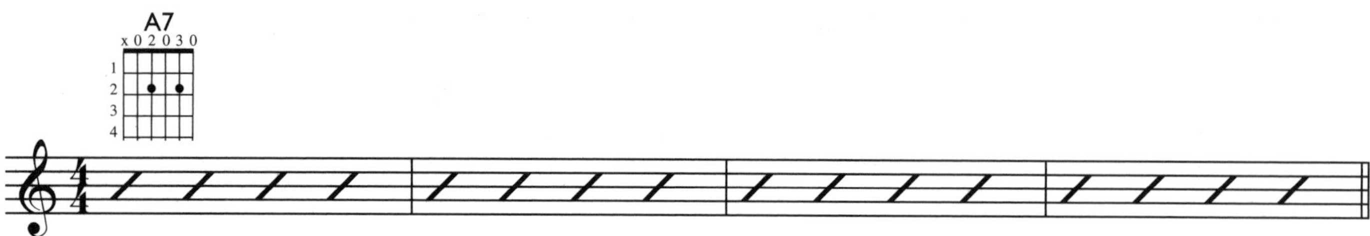


Sometimes, *rhythmic notation* is used. This is a way of conveying rhythm without pitch.

**Chord Chart (Rhythmic Notation)**

Here are the rhythmic notation values.

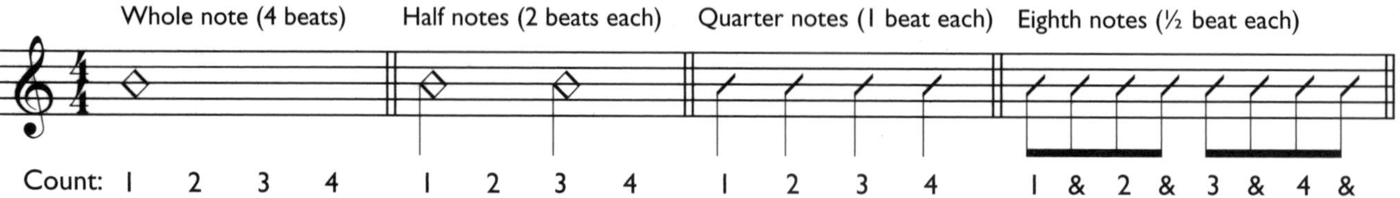


This symbol ⊓ signifies a *downstroke;* it tells us to strum or pick downward (toward the floor). This symbol V signifies an *upstroke;* it tells us to strum or pick upward (toward the ceiling). When strumming down, strike all of the chord tones. When strumming up, strike only the first few strings (those closest to the floor). The upstrums should sound lighter than the downstrums.

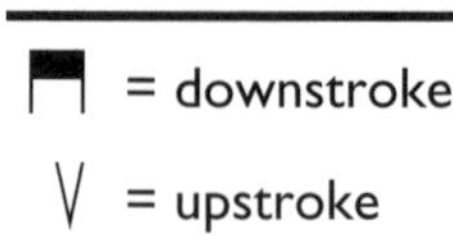


When it is assumed you know how a chord is to be played, only the chord name is given.

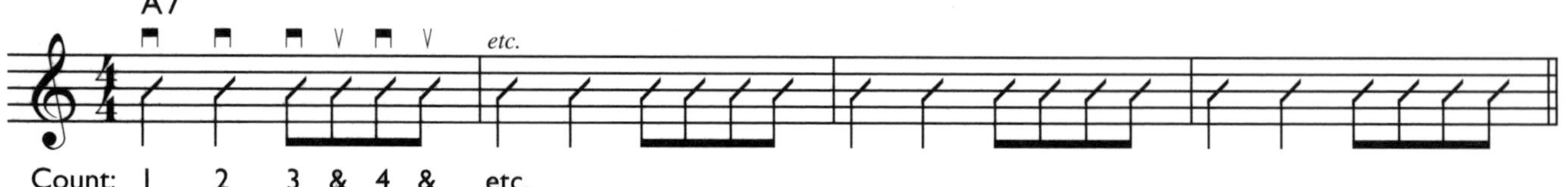

# POSTURE

Posture is very important when playing guitar. Sit or stand up straight. This will help you avoid back problems and fatigue. Do not strain; your hands, arms and shoulders should be loose and relaxed.

Here are the proper playing positions.

*Standing with guitar strap.*

*Sitting with strap.*

When sitting, use a strap to elevate the neck to a 45 degree angle, to simulate how it would be if you were standing. This will keep your wrists straight and give you easy access to the neck.

## RIGHT-HAND TECHNIQUE

There is no *one* correct right-hand approach when playing acoustic blues. One approach is to *strum* the strings. This is accomplished by moving rapidly across the strings with either the thumb or a guitar pick (also called *flatpick*). Picks come in various shapes and thicknesses. It is advisable to use a medium or heavy gauge pick in the standard triangular shape with rounded edges. The thicker the pick, the fuller the sound that is produced. You want a full, fat sound for the blues. Thinner picks work well for pop or folk/rock style strumming, but sound thin when playing single notes or blues rhythms. Some players use combinations of their thumb and fingers or even a guitar pick and fingers. Other players use a *country blues style,* which is a total *fingerpicking* approach (see page 84, Fingerstyle Blues).

*The right hand should be placed near or over the soundhole.*

Most of the exercises in this book are intended to be played with a pick. This is the most common approach and will give you an appropriate sound in most situations. However, you are also encouraged to play the exercises with your bare thumb. A pick will give you a clear sound with a hard edge. The thumb will give you a sound that is softer and rounder or "fatter." You will be a more versatile guitarist if you are accustomed to both ways of playing. It is one factor in achieving the best sound you can for each song you play.

## LEFT-HAND TECHNIQUE

When fretting the strings, place your left-hand fingers just to the left of the fret wire—never on top of it. Curve them slightly and do not press too hard. If a tone is not clear, the problem is most likely bad finger placement, not insufficient force. If your guitar seems unusually difficult to play, have a repair person take a look at it.

*A good left-hand position.*

Position your thumb in the center of the back of the neck.

*Thumb behind the neck.*

# CHAPTER 2

# 12-Bar Blues Progressions

The standard musical form used in the blues is the *12-bar blues progression.* It is 12 bars (measures) long and is almost always in $\frac{4}{4}$ time. Although there are many variations, it consists of three chords that progress in standard patterns. In this chapter, you'll learn two of the most important versions of the 12-bar blues.

## EASIEST 12-BAR BLUES

The following chord progression is the most basic 12-bar blues form and the easiest to play. Throughout this book we will refer to it as the "Easiest Blues" form.

Here are the three chords you will need to play this progression.

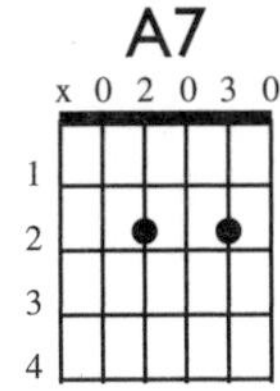


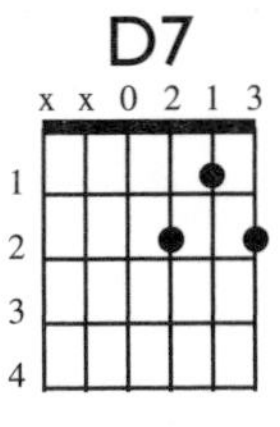


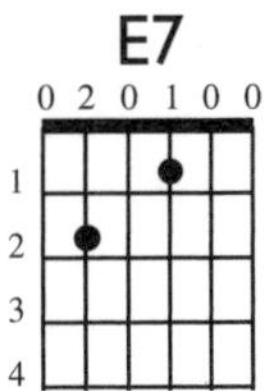


If you are unfamiliar with any of these chords, practice changing from one to another, back and forth, repeatedly. It takes time and consistent practice for new chords to become comfortable.

All the examples in this chapter are to be played with a simple quarter-note strum rhythm: one strum for each beat. With each strum, count the beat numbers aloud and tap your foot. Make sure that the beats are all equal in duration and the *tempo,* or speed, is steady and consistent.

### *EASIEST 12-BAR BLUES*

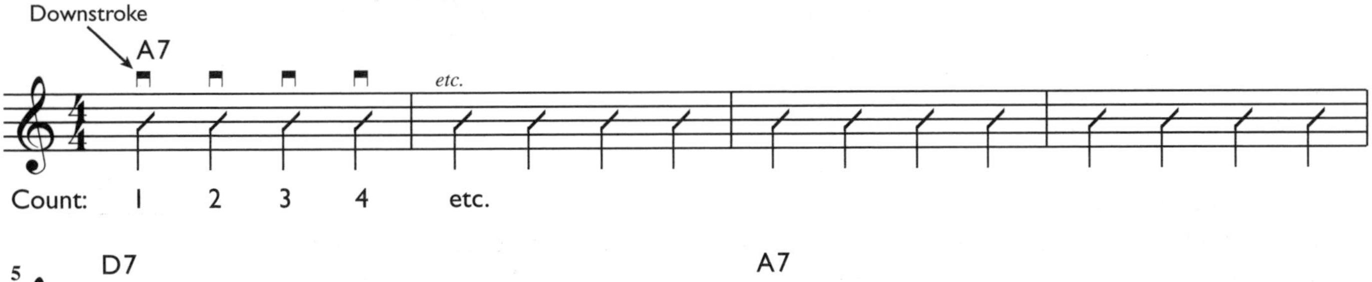

To understand what is happening musically in the blues progression you just played, let's look at some music theory.

## SCALES

A *scale* is a series of notes arranged in a specific order of whole steps and half steps. The notes of a scale ascend and descend in alphabetical order (remember, the musical alphabet is the first seven letters of the English alphabet, A through G). Each note in the scale is a *scale degree.* The scale degrees are numbered upward from the lowest note.

## MAJOR SCALES

A *major scale* is made up of eight notes with half steps between the 3rd and 4th, and 7th and 8th degrees. The distance between the rest are whole steps. The scale takes its name from its lowest note (1st degree or *tonic*). The eight notes of the scale span an octave. The 8th degree is an octave above the 1st degree. Study the placement of whole and half steps represented by the letters "W" and "H" in the example on the right.

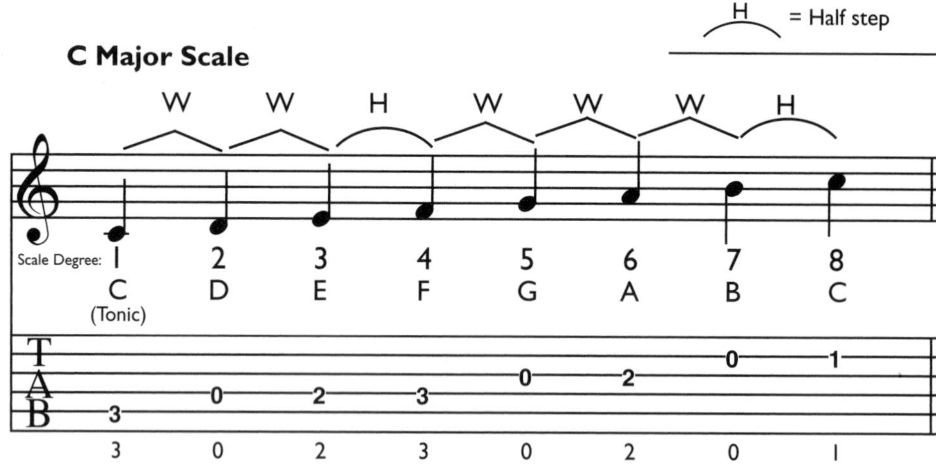


## CHORDS COME FROM SCALES

The chords we use to play the blues are derived from the major scale. Remember that a chord is three or more notes played together. We create a *triad,* the most basic kind of chord, by simply using every other note in a major scale. For example, to the right is how we build a C Major chord:

In the blues, we usually need only three chords for any tune: a chord built on the 1st degree (the *I* chord—Roman numerals are used to refer to chords), the 4th degree (the *IV* chord) and the 5th degree (the *V* chord). In the illustration to the right, these chords are shown in the *key* (the set of notes and chords of a scale) of C:

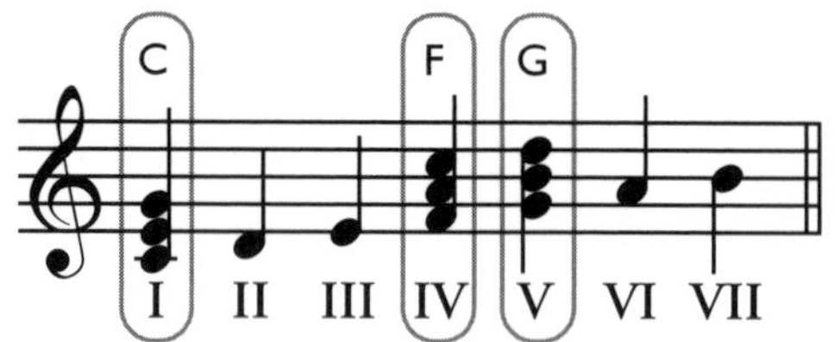


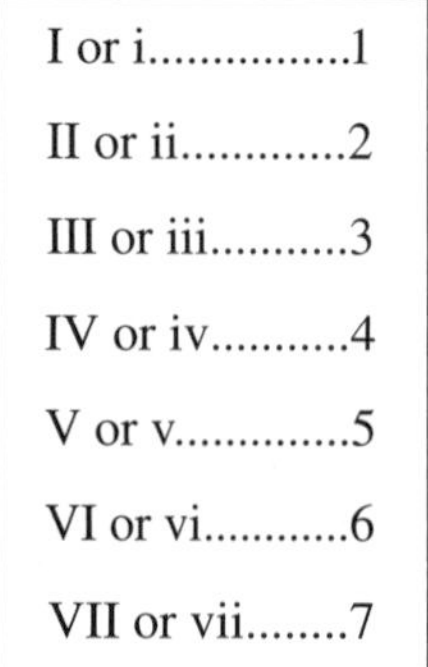

| | |
|---|---|
| I or i | 1 |
| II or ii | 2 |
| III or iii | 3 |
| IV or iv | 4 |
| V or v | 5 |
| VI or vi | 6 |
| VII or vii | 7 |

## EASIEST BLUES FORM—ANALYSIS

The Easiest 12-Bar Blues (page 19) is in the key of A, which means the notes of the melody and the chords are all from the A Major scale. The chords built from the 1st, 4th and 5th scale degrees are A7(I), D7(IV) and E7(V). Note that in the blues, chords are often made into "7" chords (covered in detail on pages 38–39) for more of a bluesy feel.

The Easiest Blues form should be memorized, as it is the standard form for the 12-bar blues. It consists of:

- Four bars of I
- Two bars of IV
- Two bars of I
- Two bars of V
- Two bars of I

Now let's play this same progression in the key of E. This is the most common of all blues keys. The pattern for the Roman numerals are the same, but the chords themselves are different. The I, IV and V—or *primary chords*—in the key of E are E7(I), A7(IV) and B7(V).

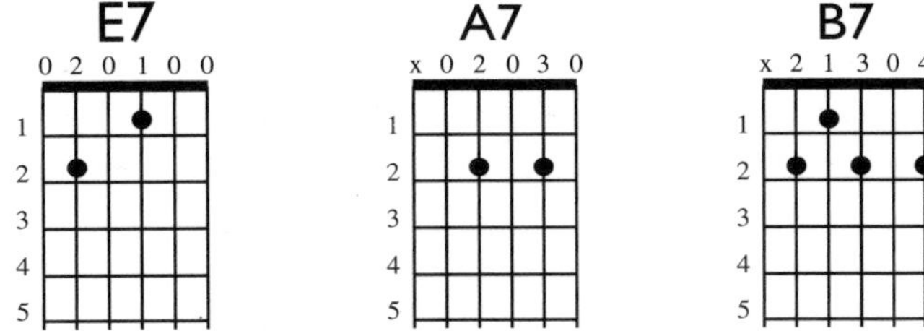


Work on the B7 chord for awhile. It can be challenging at first because you are fretting a note with your 4th finger, but you need to master this very common blues chord.

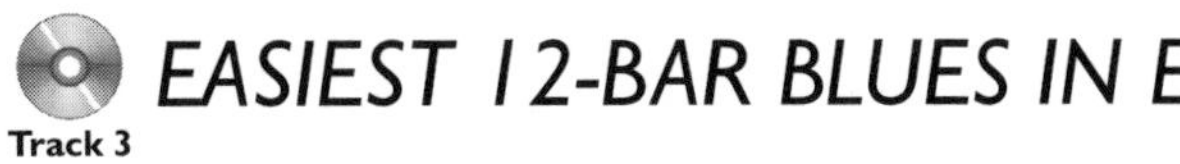


## EASIEST 12-BAR BLUES IN E

### BACKBEAT

In the blues (as well as rock and other popular styles), all beats are not created equal. Most blues tunes are in $\frac{4}{4}$, with four beats per bar. To create a rhythmic pulse, accent (or strum louder on) the 2nd and 4th beats in each bar. This emphasis on the 2nd and 4th beats is called a *backbeat*. It should be your standard approach throughout this book.

# MOST COMMON 12-BAR BLUES

Chord movements in songs are called *changes*. The most common 12-bar blues progression —referred to throughout this book as the "Most Common Blues"—has a few more changes than the Easiest Blues form. There is a quick change from the I chord in the 1st bar to the IV chord in the 2nd bar and back again to the I in the 3rd bar. This is called a *quick IV*. There are other changes in the last four bars as well.

The repeat sign in the 12th measure tells us to repeat the progression from the beginning and then play the last two bars. Of course, at a gig or at a jam session, you'll be playing through any progression more than twice. The 12-bar progression is repeated numerous times as a singer sings and musicians solo. Each run through the 12-bar form is a *chorus*. At the very end, we usually add a bar or two of the I chord to give a sense of finality to the piece.

## *MOST COMMON 12-BAR BLUES IN A*

Track 4

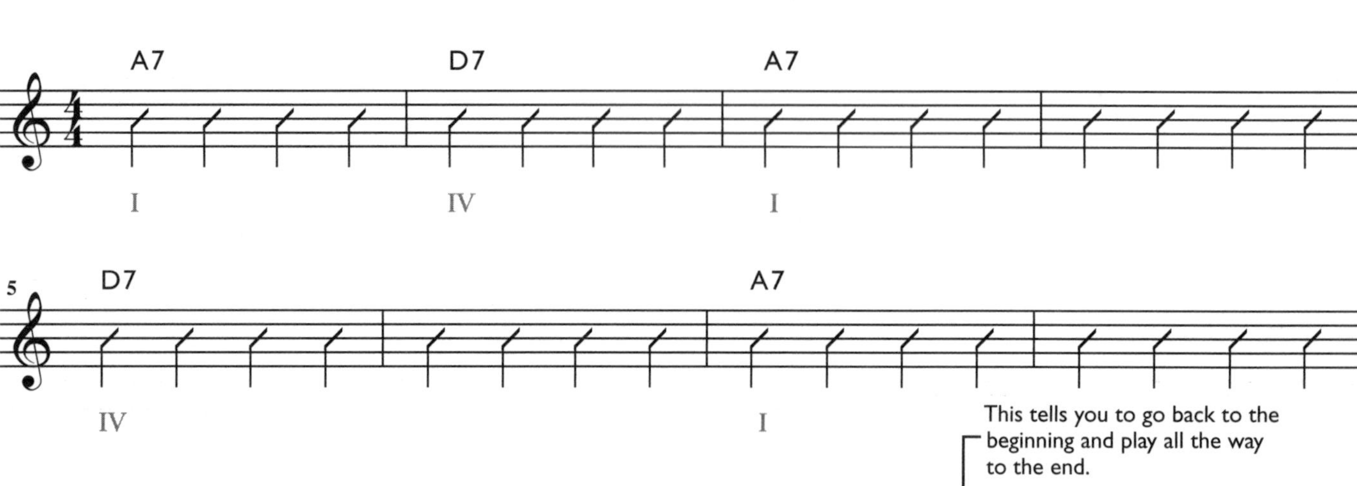


To summarize, the Most Common Blues progression consists of:

- One bar of I
- One bar of IV
- Two bars of I
- Two bars of IV
- Two bars of I
- One bar of V
- One bar of IV
- One bar of I
- One bar of V
- At the very end, two bars of I

This should also be memorized as it is the most widely used form of the 12-bar blues.

Now let's play the Most Common Blues form in the key of E. It is important to memorize the Easiest and Most Common Blues forms in the keys of A and E and, eventually, all the common keys.

## MOST COMMON 12-BAR BLUES IN E

Track 5

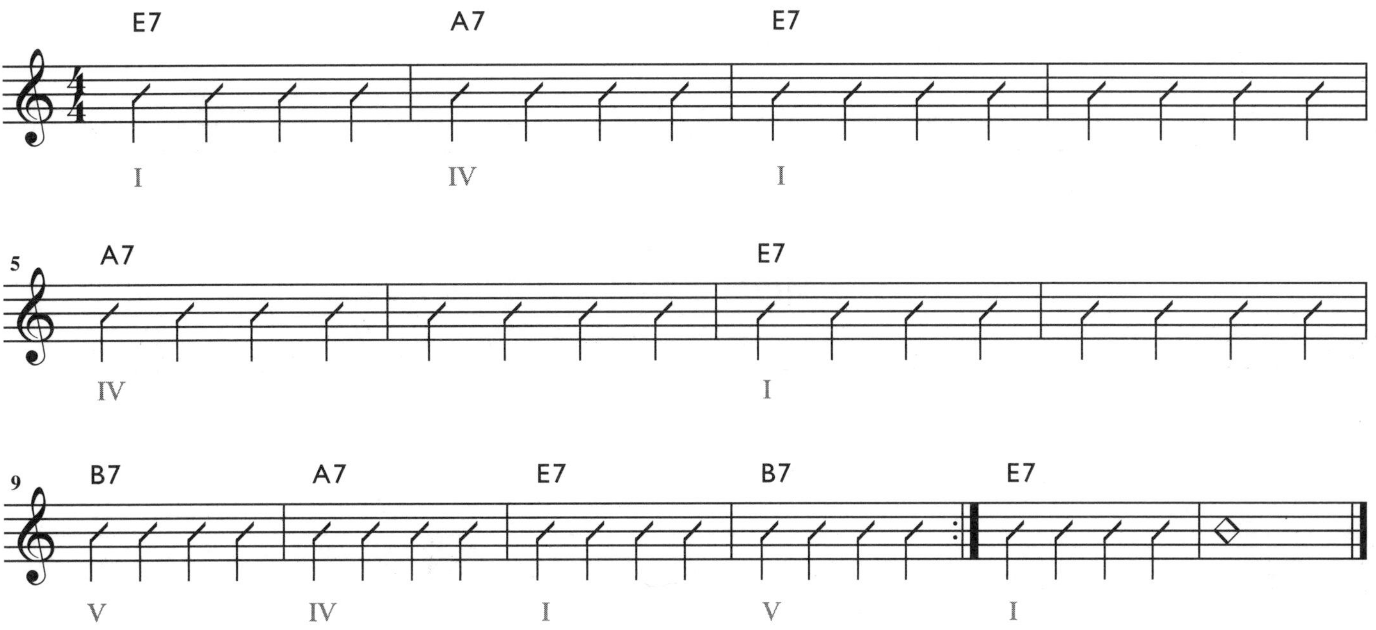


Notice that, though the chords are different from the progression in the key of A, the Roman numeral pattern is the same.

COURTESY OF STAR FILE PHOTO, INC. PHOTO BY PICTORIAL

*Son House (1902-1988). His song "Death Letter" is a classic example of the Delta Blues style, which is often characterized by a solo singer accompanying himself on a guitar. The blues historian Alan Lomax recorded Son House in 1941 in Lake Coromont, Mississippi for the Library of Congress archives.*

While the keys of A and E are the most popular for guitar-based blues, there are other keys that are widely used as well.

The primary chords in the key of D are D7(I), G7(IV) and A7(V).

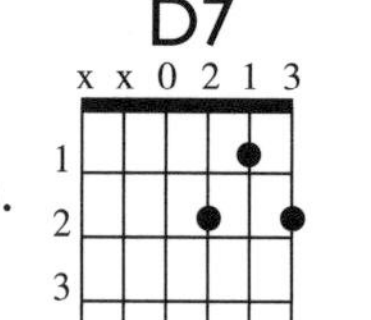


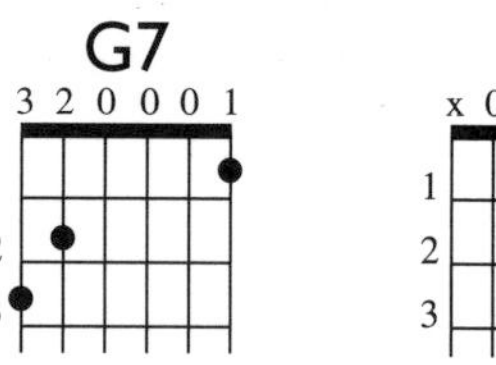

## MOST COMMON 12-BAR BLUES IN D

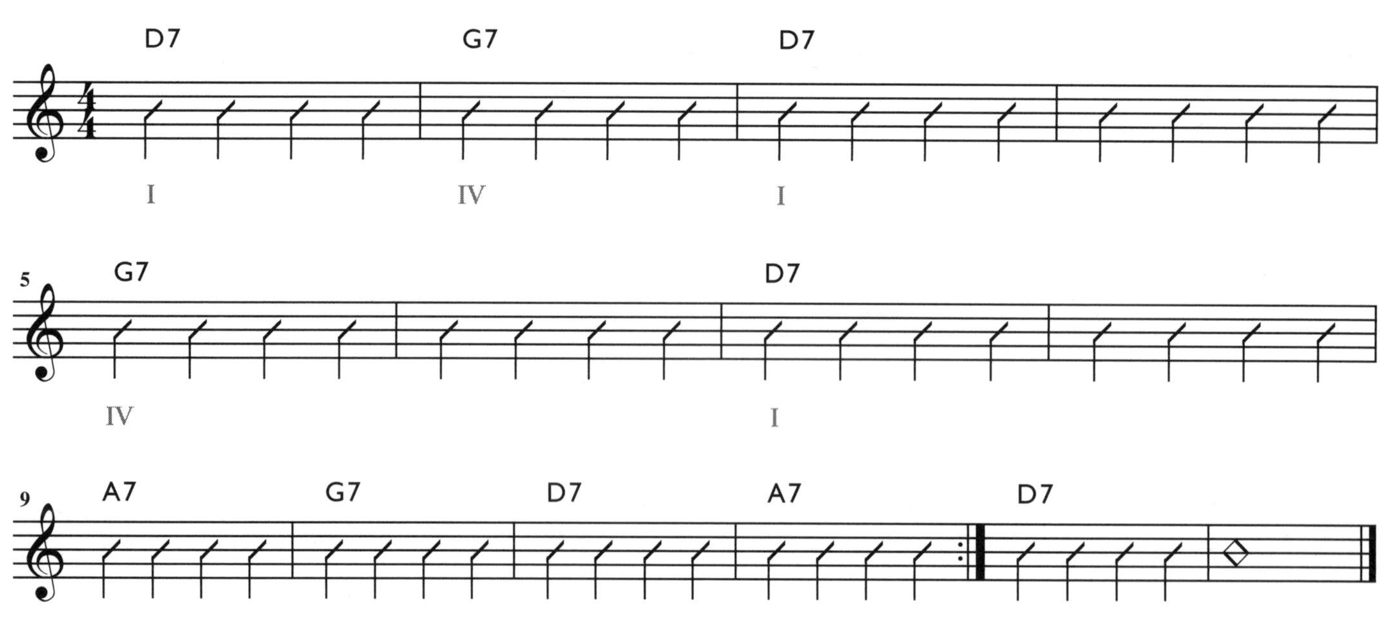


The primary chords in the key of G are G7(I), C7(IV) and D7(V).

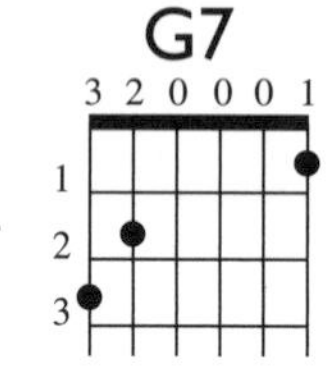


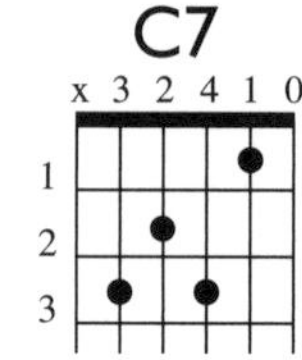


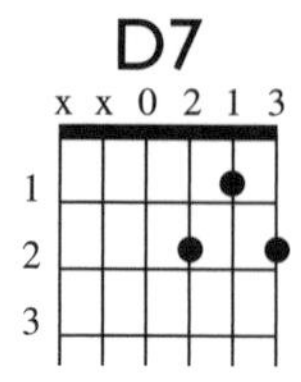

## MOST COMMON 12-BAR BLUES IN G

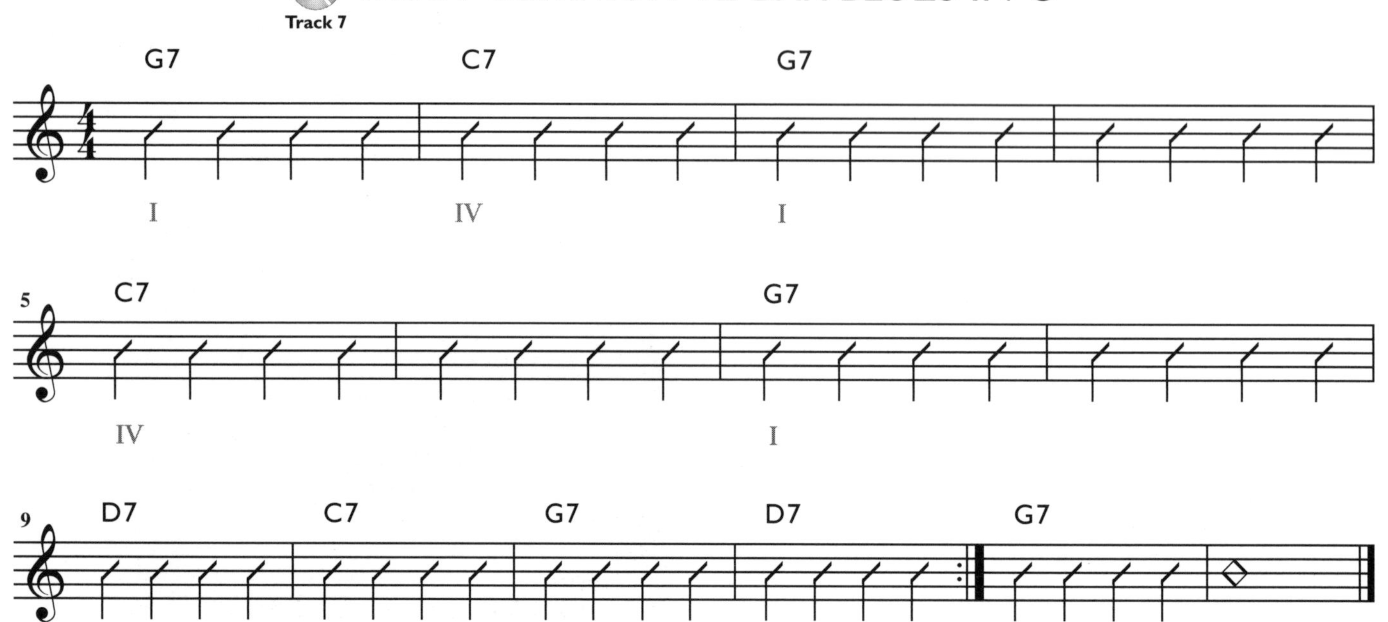

# CHAPTER 3

# Blues Rhythm & Theory

## SWING EIGHTHS

In blues (and jazz also), eighth notes are not usually played exactly as notated. Rather, they are interpreted in what is called a *swing* or *shuffle* style. This makes a pair of eighth notes sound like the first and last notes of a triplet (page 13). This is important to know, since almost every example in this book is in swing style. *Swing eighths* look exactly like "straight eighths," but we play them in swing style. In this book, this swing rhythm is indicated with the caption: *Swing 8ths.*

Written and counted: Played:

If you were to run down the street, the rhythm your feet make would be straight eighths. If you were to skip down the street, you would be skipping with a swing or shuffle rhythm, where the first step of each pair is longer than the second: long-short, long-short, long-short. So try running and skipping down the street and just tell your friends you are practicing blues rhythm!

## INTERVALS

The major scale is the standard by which many musical concepts can be understood. To use the scale this way, it is important to understand *intervals.* An interval is the distance between two pitches. You already know two intervals: the whole step and the half step.

Every pitch in a major scale can be understood in terms of its interval from the tonic. The second degree, for example, is an interval of a 2nd (2) above the tonic. The third degree is an interval of a 3rd (3) above the tonic, and so on. The same note sounded more than once is a *unison.*

P = Perfect
M = Major

Every interval has a *quality.* It is either *major, minor, perfect, diminished* or *augmented.* All of the pitches in a major scale, when measured from the tonic, create perfect or major intervals.

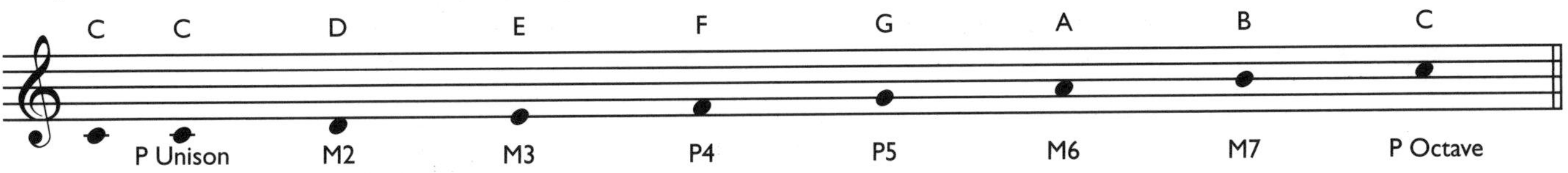


A major interval can be changed to a minor interval using an accidental. For example, C–E is a major 3rd, so C–E♭ is a minor 3rd. Other intervals can be changed this way, too.

# CHAPTER 4

## Blues Shuffles

Until now, we have played the Easiest and Most Common Blues progressions with quarter-note strums: one strum for every beat. This works fine in many cases. Knowing when to keep it simple is important in the blues. But you need to learn other important rhythms as well. *Shuffle style,* which is played with swing eighths (page 25) is one of the most widely used rhythms in blues, rock and even country music.

## TWO-STRING CHORDS

### "5" CHORDS

A *5 chord* is made up of two notes on the lower strings. They are really just *intervals* of a perfect 5th (see page 25). To the right is a diagram of an A5 chord. Its two notes are A on the open 5th string, and E on the 2nd fret of the 4th string. In an A Major scale, A is the 1st scale degree and E is the 5th. Because of this, it is called A5.

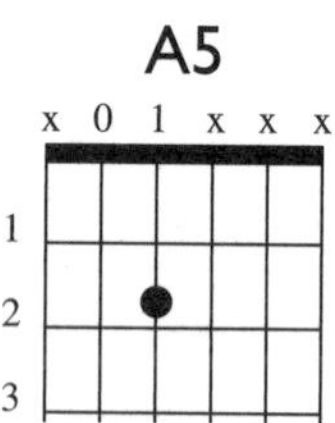


It's common for players to base their entire approach around these chords, as with punk, hard rock or metal styles. They create a strong sound and in this context they are called *power chords.*

With all two-string chords, be sure to strum only the two strings that are indicated. This can be a little tricky at first, but if you are hitting unwanted strings, you will not get the right sound. You can mute the 3rd string by leaning your 1st finger against it.

Play the exercise below—and all the pieces in this chapter—using downstrokes only; it's the standard approach for this two-string style. Also, be sure to tap your foot on the onbeats (the numbers) and count: 1–&, 2–&, 3–&, 4–&, etc.

Remember, this is played with swing eighths, so the eighth notes are more like the first and last notes of an eighth-note triplet.

A *key signature* is at the beginning of every line of music and tells you which notes are sharp or flat throughout the piece. You can tell what key you are in by the number of sharps or flats. The key of A has three sharps.

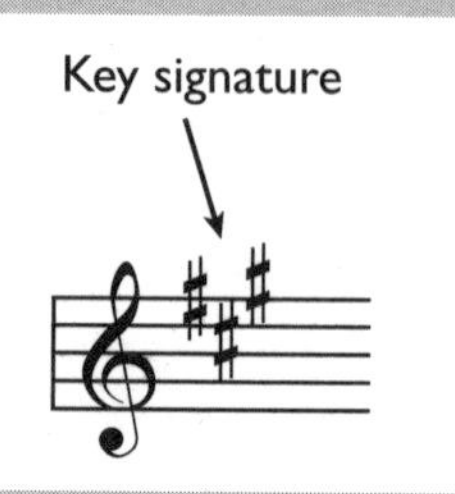


Key signature

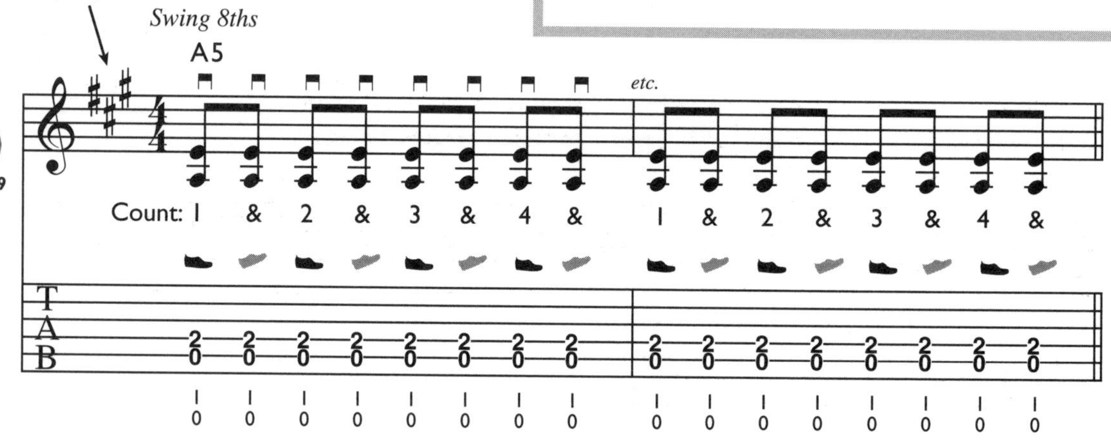

## "6" CHORDS

We can now tweak these "5" chords by moving the fretted note one whole step up on the fretboard. This new note is the interval of a major 6th from the bottom note so it is called a "6" chord. For example, to the right is a diagram of an A6 chord. It consists of A on the open 5th string and F♯ on the 4th fret of the 4th string. In an A Major scale, A is the 1st scale degree and F♯ is the 6th. Because of this, it is called A6.

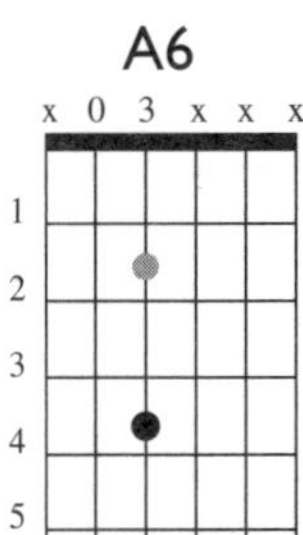


Notice that the A6 chord diagram to the right shows two notes fretted on the 4th string. The gray dot is telling you to keep your 1st finger on the 2nd fret while also fretting the 4th fret with your 3rd finger. Although the E on the 2nd fret will not be heard when fretting the F♯ on the 4th fret, you'll be alternating between the "5" and "6" forms.

Below is an exercise to get you started with this.

3
Track 10

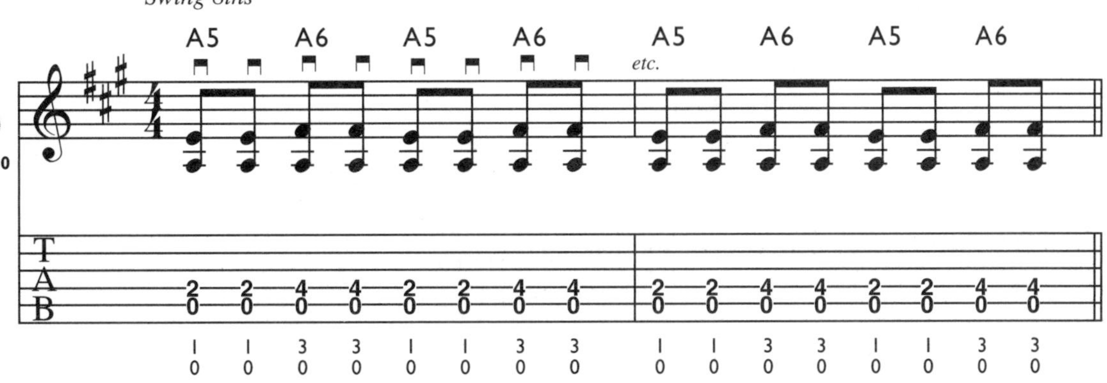

PHOTO COURTESY OF BANNING EYRE

*Taj Mahal (born Henry St. Clair Fredericks) was a major force in the blues revival of the 1960s. A champion of traditional acoustic blues, he has also infused his unique style with roots and folk music from all over the world.*

Let's apply this technique to the 4th and 3rd strings. This gives us D5 and D6.

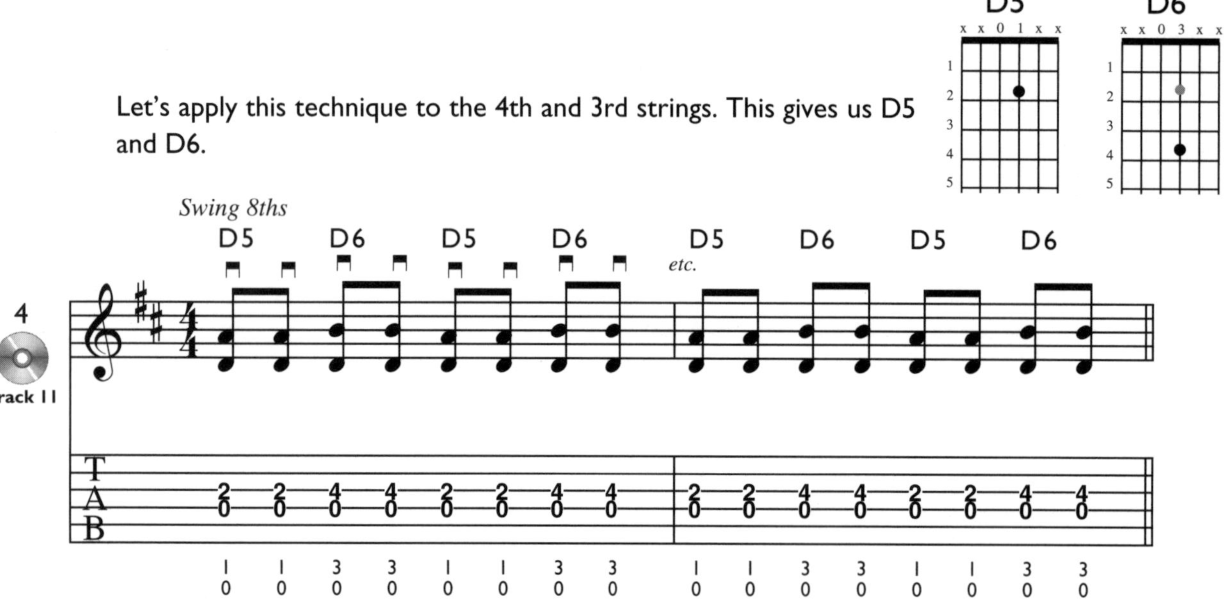


Now let's apply this to the 6th and 5th strings. This gives us E5 and E6.

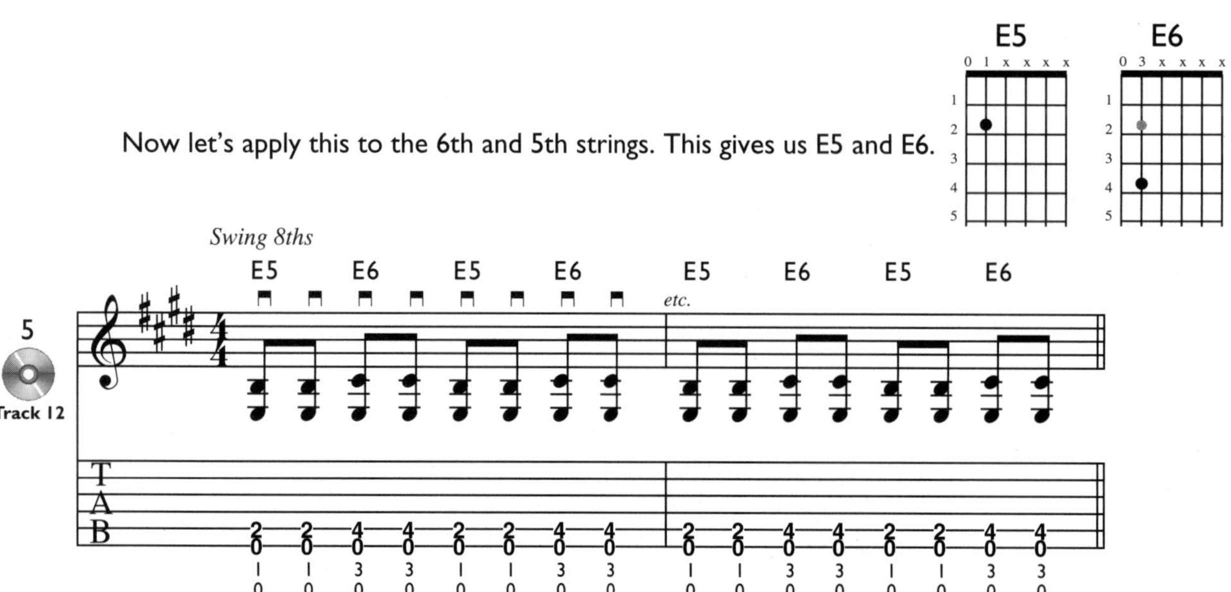


Every leading blues artist has played in this style. Some, like Jimmy Reed, have used it in almost all of their songs.

Normally, in songs featuring this two-string shuffle style, only the general chord sound is written above the staff. So, instead of an alternating A5–A6–A5–A6, you will see only A.

Now let's apply this technique to an entire blues form. Below is the Easiest Blues played in this cool double-note shuffle style.

*Chords in gray show the general sound of the music and are not necessarily meant to be played.*

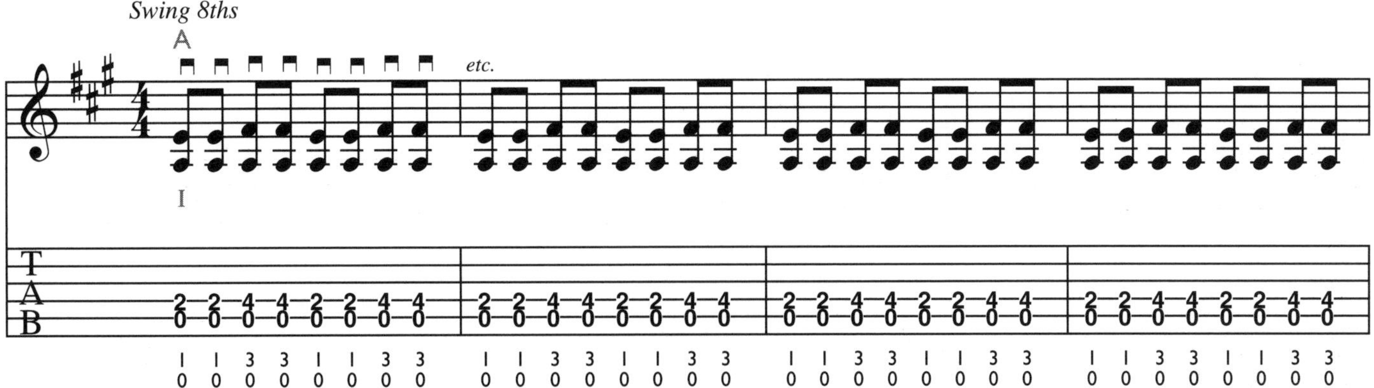


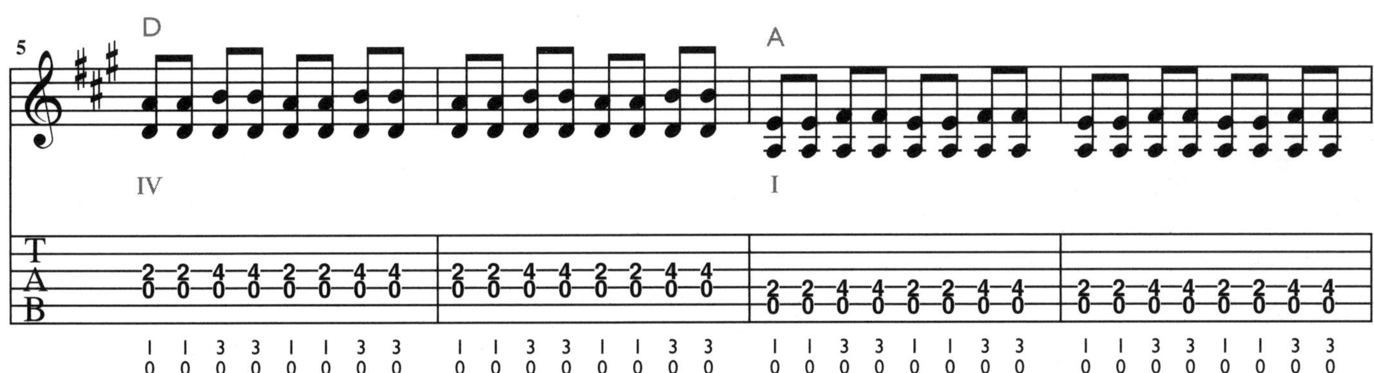


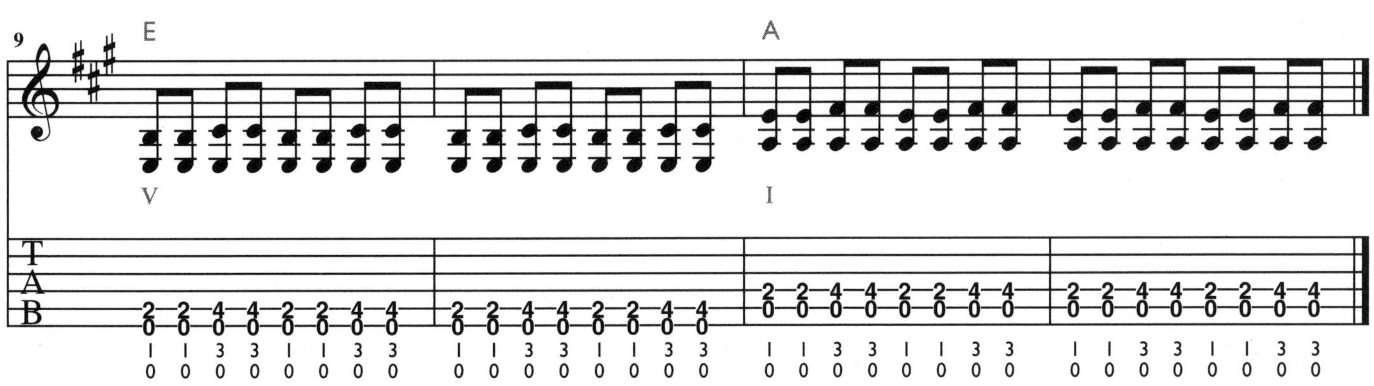

### THE FLAT-7

We use the term "flat" loosely in this context to mean "lower a half step." For example, if we flat a G♯, we get a G♮. G♯ is the 7th scale degree in the A Major scale, so G♮ is considered a ♭7 (flat-7).

Below is a variation on the alternating "5" and "6" chord pattern. If you use the 4th finger of your left hand to go one fret higher than the 6th, you will be playing a ♭7. This is an essential blues sound.

This shuffle uses the Most Common Blues form.

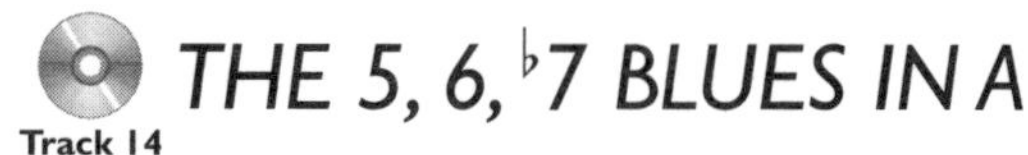


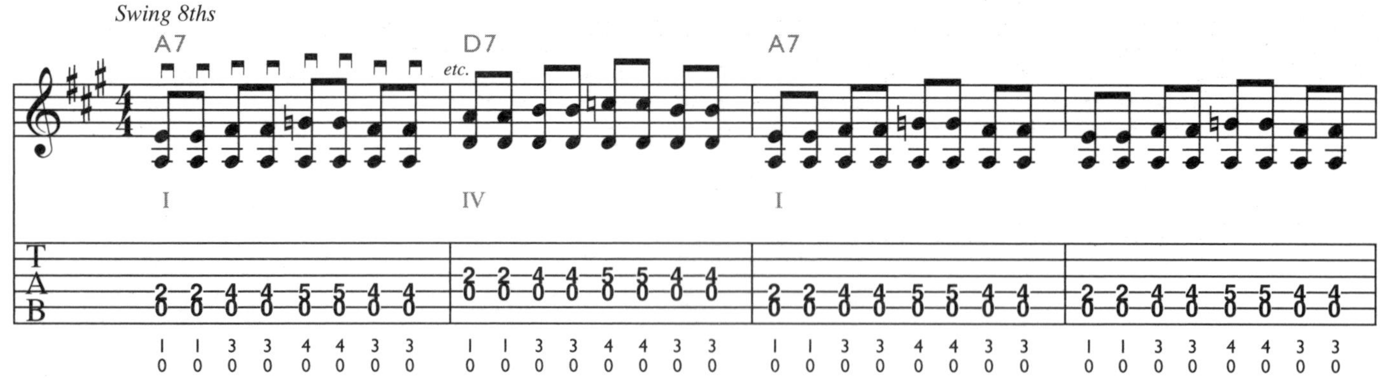


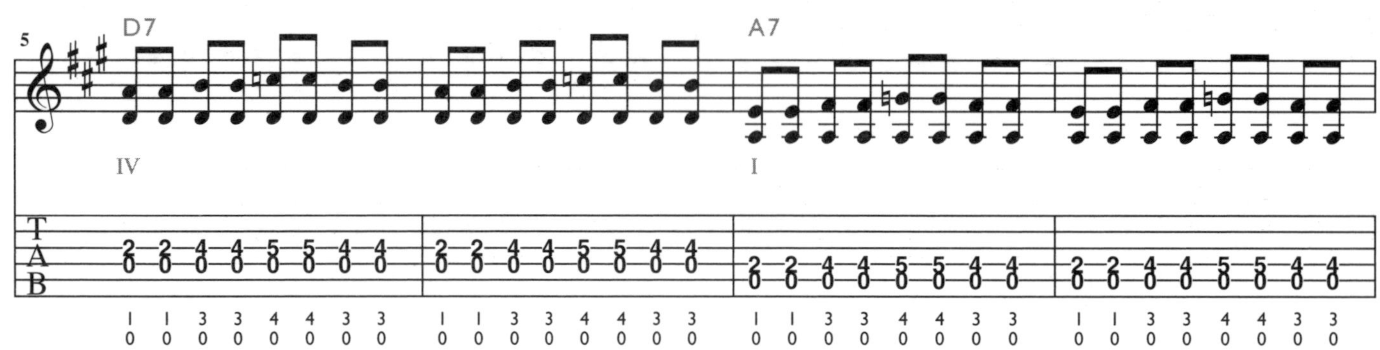


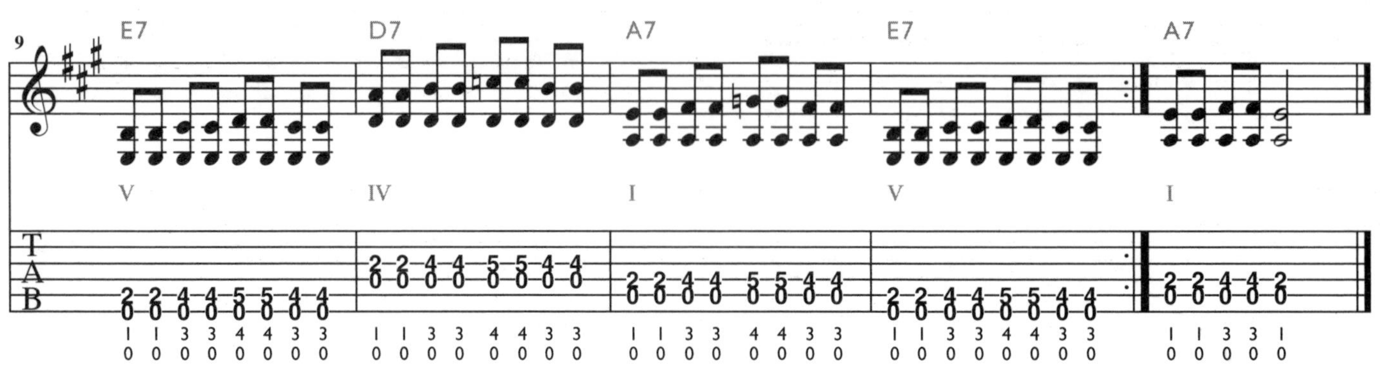

The following piece is a Most Common Blues in the key of E. It combines two-string variations of "5," "6" and "♭7" chords with full chords. Strum the full chords in bars 9, 10 and 12 with a down-up pattern. Strum all the strings in the chord on the downstrokes, but give less emphasis to the upstrokes, strumming only the first few strings. Notice in the last measure that, in TAB, tied notes are in parentheses.

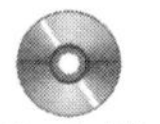

Track 15

## SHUFFLE BLUES IN E

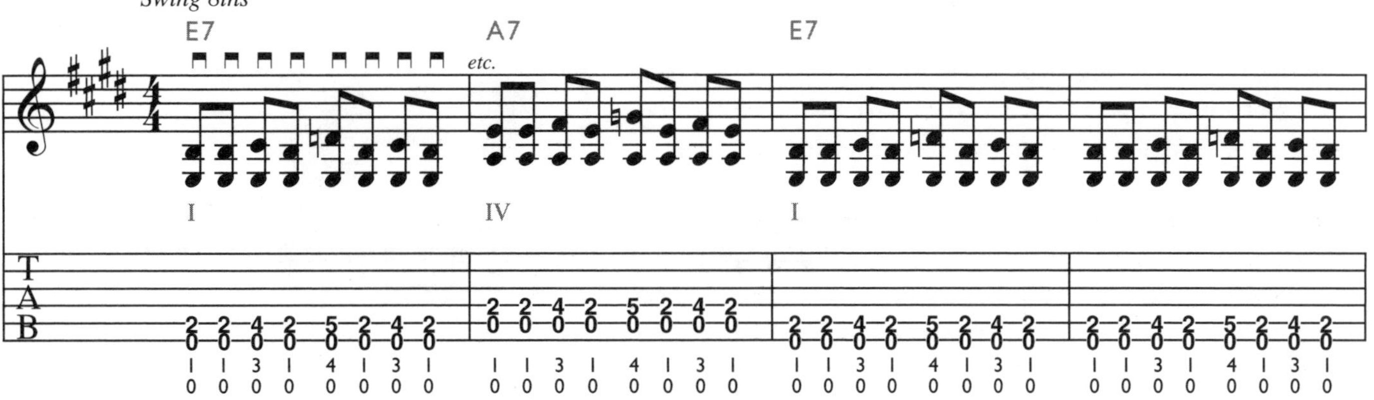


5

A7 E7

IV I

9

B7 A7 E7 B7

etc.

V IV I V

In TAB, tied notes are in parentheses.

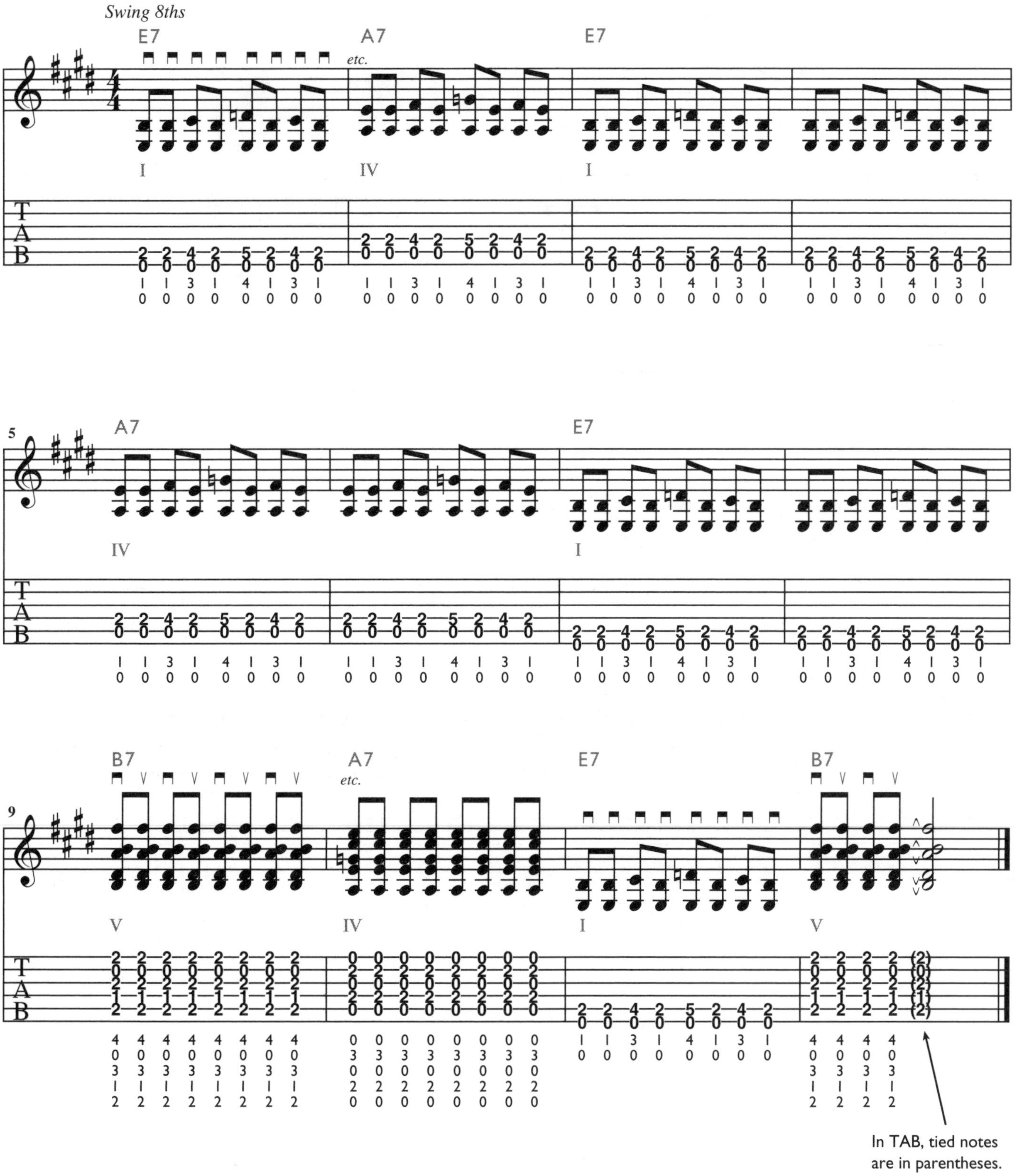

# CHAPTER 5

## Palm Muting

Now that you've played your first blues shuffle, let's look at a right-hand technique that is used very often in this style. It's called *palm muting* and is quite easy once you get the hang of it.

For this technique, your hand must be positioned at the *bridge* (the piece that is glued to the front part of the guitar body, where the strings are anchored—see photo to the right).

*Right-hand position for palm muting.*

Notice that the strings go right over the *saddle* (the thin white plastic piece that sits on the bridge). Place the lower left part, or *heel,* of your right hand on the saddle where the lower strings rest. Do not press too hard. Just rest your hand. We merely want to dampen the sound of the strings, not cut them out entirely.

Experiment with the pressure and placement. Don't go too far back or too far forward. You should be resting right where the strings hit the saddle.

Use this new technique on the example below. Try to match the sound on the CD. It's a sound you've heard on many a blues, rock and country tune.

P.M.= Palm mute

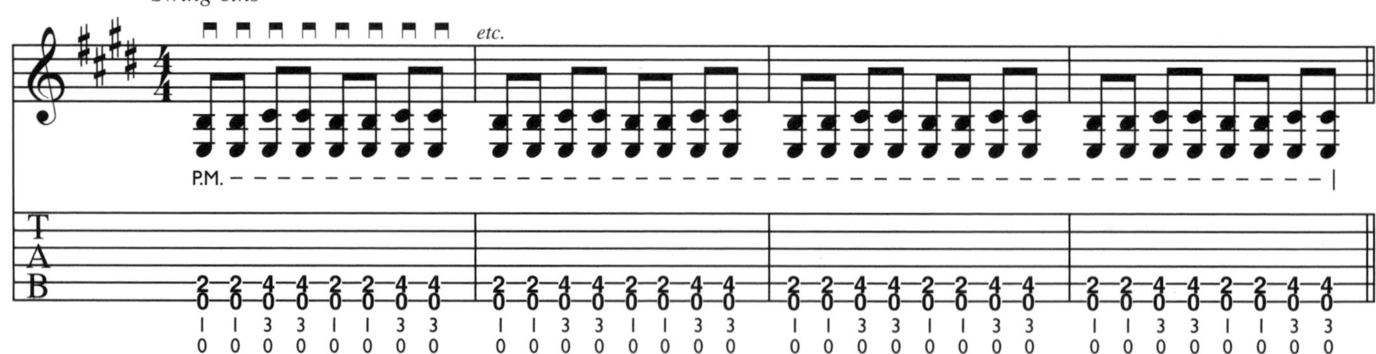

The next piece uses the Most Common Blues form. It uses a variation on the alternating "5" and "6" chord pattern. In each group of four strums, you strum the "5" chord twice, then the "6" chord once, then the "5" chord once more. So the pattern is 5–5–6–5, 5–5–6–5, etc.

Because we are using straight eighths rather than swing eighths, it is not considered a shuffle. Many blues tunes use this steady rhythm rather than the shuffle rhythm. You need to be able to play in swing and steady eighth-note style, and to feel the difference between the two rhythms. This can be challenging for many beginning players. A way to develop this ability is to listen to—and play along with—the CD that accompanies this book. Also, when listening to other music, try to distinguish whether the rhythm is in swing or straight-eighth style.

## PALM MUTING IN A

Track 17

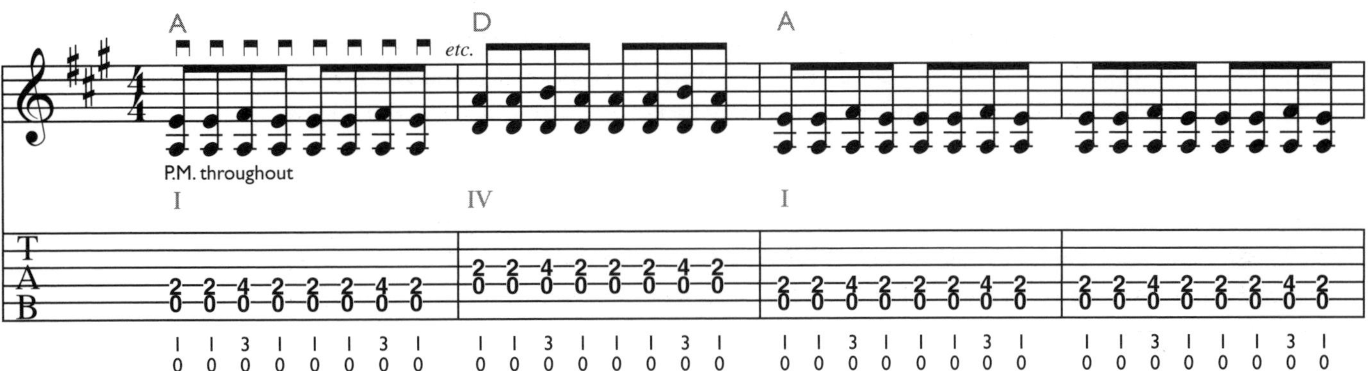


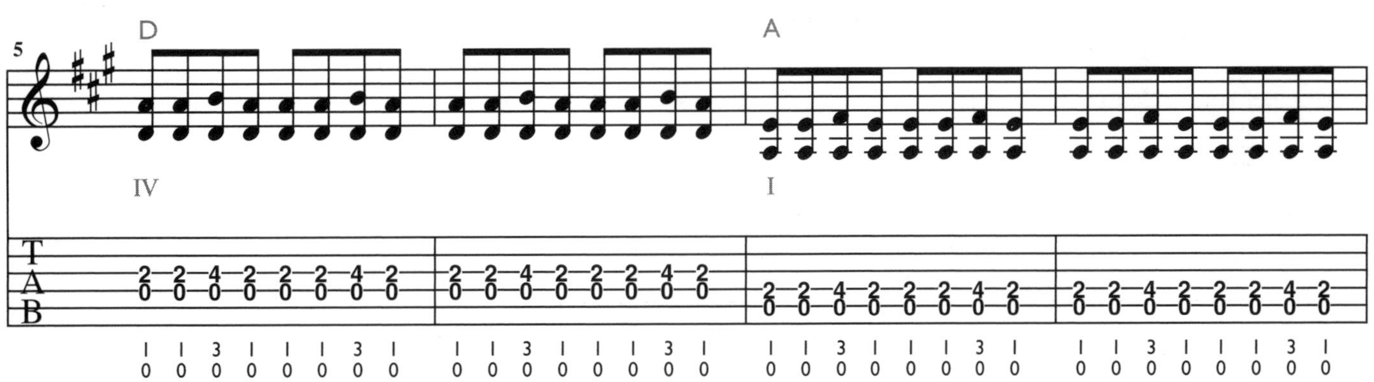


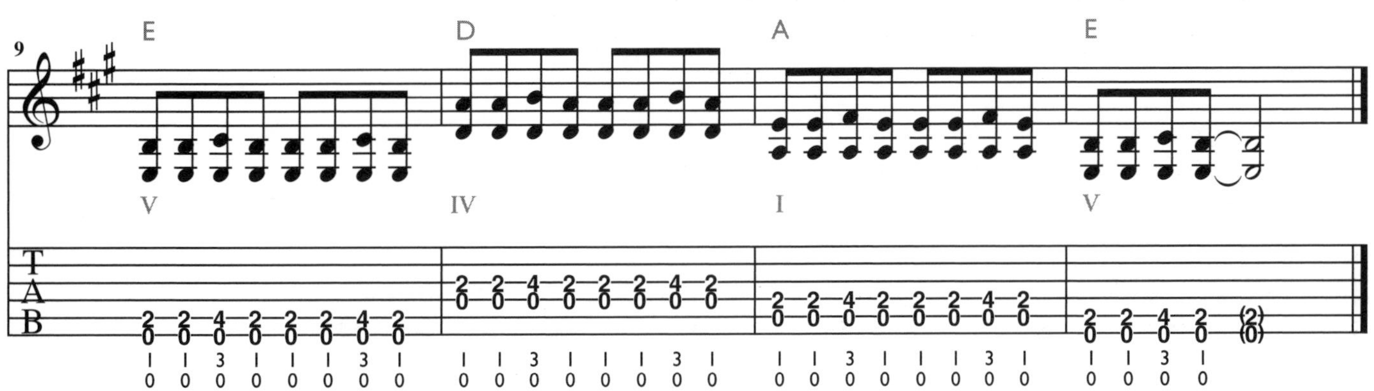

# CHAPTER 6

# Major Scale Theory Review

We have already taken our first look at the major scale (page 20). Because it is the standard by which we can understand many other musical concepts, we must now take a closer look.

Oddly enough, it is more important for a blues player to know major scale theory than to be able to play major scales on the guitar. The reason for this is that they are generally not used in the blues style.

Remember, a scale is a series of notes arranged in a particular pattern of whole steps and half steps. The major scale is made up of a series of seven notes. The note that follows the 7th note, or scale degree, is the octave of the tonic. You may be familiar with this scale in the form of the famous "doh–re–mi–fa–so–la–ti–doh" sequence.

As you learned on page 20, the major scale is made up of whole steps and half steps in this order: **W**hole–**W**hole–**H**alf–**W**hole–**W**hole–**W**hole–**H**alf, or **W–W–H–W–W–W–H.** The sentence "**W**endy **W**itch **H**as **W**ild **W**onderful **W**avy **H**air" can help you remember this pattern of whole and half steps.

If we start this pattern for a major scale with C as our tonic, our notes are C–D–E–F–G–A–B–C.

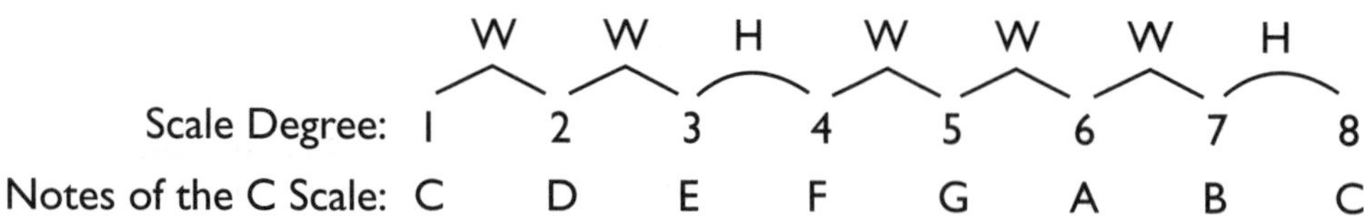


W = Whole step

H = Half step

Let's play the C Major scale. Here it is in standard music notation and TAB.

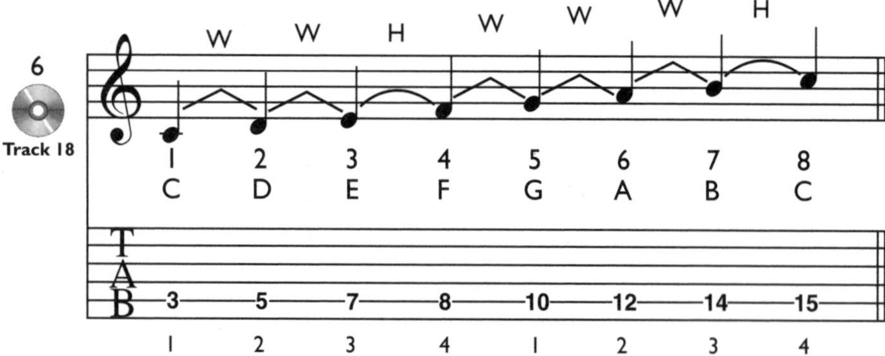


Here is a fretboard diagram of the C Major scale on one string.

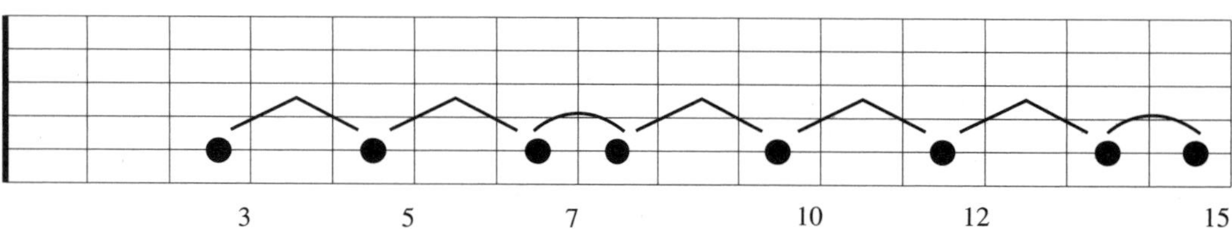

A major scale, like any scale, can start on any note. The chart below contains the notes for almost every major scale.

Scale degrees →

These scales are enharmonic equivalents. (F♯ and G♭ rows)

| The Major Scale | | | | | | | |
|---|---|---|---|---|---|---|---|
| 1 | 2 | 3 | 4 | 5 | 6 | 7 | 8 |
| C | D | E | F | G | A | B | C |
| G | A | B | C | D | E | F♯ | G |
| D | E | F♯ | G | A | B | C♯ | D |
| A | B | C♯ | D | E | F♯ | G♯ | A |
| E | F♯ | G♯ | A | B | C♯ | D♯ | E |
| B | C♯ | D♯ | E | F♯ | G♯ | A♯ | B |
| F♯ | G♯ | A♯ | B | C♯ | D♯ | E♯ | F♯ |
| G♭ | A♭ | B♭ | C♭ | D♭ | E♭ | F | G♭ |
| D♭ | E♭ | F | G♭ | A♭ | B♭ | C | D♭ |
| A♭ | B♭ | C | D♭ | E♭ | F | G | A♭ |
| E♭ | F | G | A♭ | B♭ | C | D | E♭ |
| B♭ | C | D | E♭ | F | G | A | B♭ |
| F | G | A | B♭ | C | D | E | F |

Though the F♯ Major and G♭ Major scales have different names, they sound exactly the same. These two scales consist of notes that share the same pitches, but have different names. Remember, when two notes have the same pitch, but different names, they are enharmonic equivalents (see page 8, Accidentals) .

# CHAPTER 7

# Chord Theory and Key Signatures

With our understanding of the major scale, we can now take a closer look at how chords are built and how they fit into different keys. It may be helpful to review page 25 (Intervals) before reading this chapter.

## MAJOR AND MINOR TRIADS

Remember, a chord is the combination of three (or more) different notes. The most basic chords are three-note chords called triads. *Major* and *minor triads* are the most commonly used chords. Keep in mind that the word "major" is only *implied* when talking about major chords. For example, if you are talking about a G Major chord, you would call it a "G" chord. Triads are built by stacking pitches in 3rds.

Let's build a C Major triad. C is the *root* (1) of the chord; E is a 3rd above C, so it is called the 3rd (3) of the chord; G is a 3rd above E and 5th above C, so it is called the 5th (5) of the chord. Like all major triads, it consists of a major 3rd on the bottom and a minor 3rd on the top.

M = Major
m = Minor

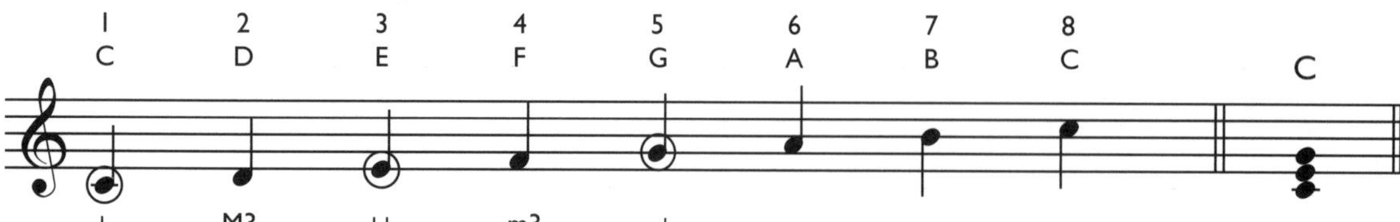


You can use the 1, 3 and 5 of any major scale to build a major triad. Lower the 3rd (♭3) of any major triad, or you can think in terms of lowering the 3rd of the scale, and you have a minor triad. Notice that it is a minor 3rd from the 1 to the ♭3 and a major 3rd from the ♭3 to the 5.

## DIMINISHED AND AUGMENTED TRIADS

A = Augmented
d = Diminished

Though they are not used as often as the major and minor, there are two other kinds of triads: *diminished* and *augmented.* A diminished triad consists of two minor 3rds and an augmented triad consists of two major 3rds. In a diminished triad, the 5th is a diminished 5th (or ♭5), or "d5." In an augmented triad the 5th is an augmented 5th (or ♯5), or "A5."

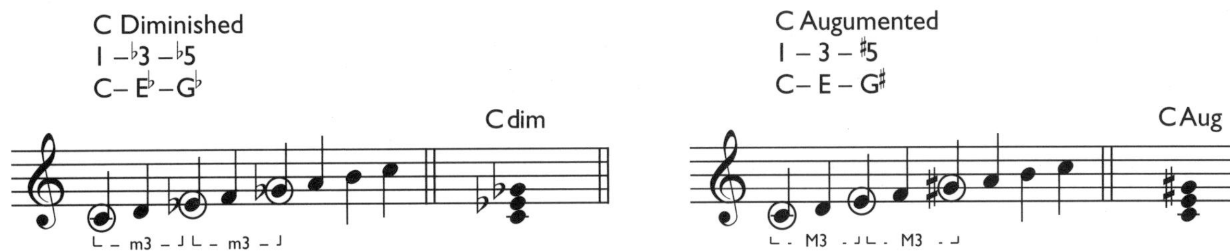


So, to get a diminished chord (abbreviated as *dim,* or designated with this symbol ○) lower the 5th of a minor triad a half step. To get an augmented chord (abbreviated as *Aug,* or designated with this symbol +), raise the 5th of a major triad a half step.

**Chord Voicings**
A *voicing* is the way the notes of a chord are stacked or arranged. So far in this chapter, we've looked at simple three-note chords. In common practice, some of these notes are doubled or even tripled in different octaves. This gives us a fuller sound than a three-note voicing.

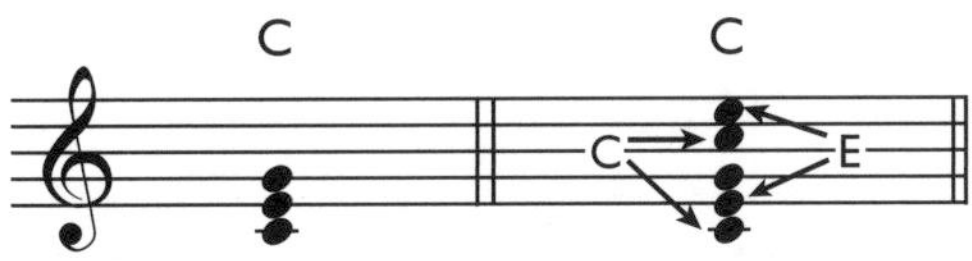

*Jimmy Reed had a sweet and easily accessible sound that has been widely appreciated and imitated. Playing harp in a mouth rack as he played guitar, he had hit after hit on the R&B and pop charts in the 1960s. This was a rare feat by a pure bluesman which has perhaps only been surpassed by B. B. King. His sweet, yearning vocals and relaxed, laid-back blues have inspired many rock bands and solo acoustic artists.*

PHOTO COURTESY OF HOHNER, INC.

## 7 CHORDS

A "7" chord is built by stacking another 3rd on top of an existing triad. The interval from the root to this added note is a 7th. So the intervals of a 7 chord are 1–3–5–7.

There are many types of 7 chords. We'll look at those most commonly used in the blues.

### MAJOR 7 CHORDS

A *major* 7 chord (Maj7) is made by placing a major 3rd above a major triad. This additional note is the interval of a major 7th (M7) from the root. The intervals of this chord are 1–3–5–7.

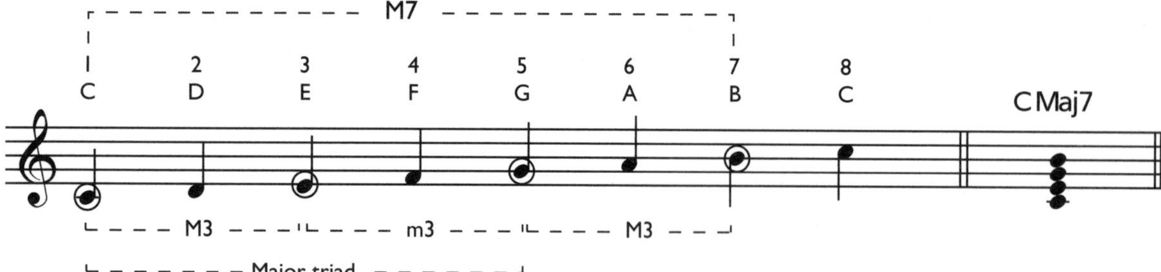


### MINOR 7 CHORDS

A *minor* 7 chord (min7) is made by placing a minor 3rd above a minor triad. This additional note is the interval of a minor 7th (m7) from the root. The intervals of this chord are 1–♭3–5–♭7.

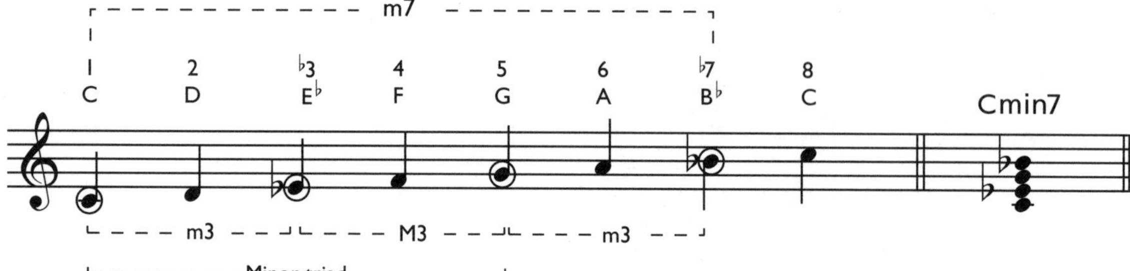


### DOMINANT 7 CHORDS

The most commonly used 7 chord in the blues is the *dominant* 7. A dominant 7 chord is designated by a "7" (for example, A7, D7 and G7). It is made by placing a minor 3rd above a major triad. This additional note is the interval of a minor 7th from the root. The intervals of this chord are 1–3–5–♭7.

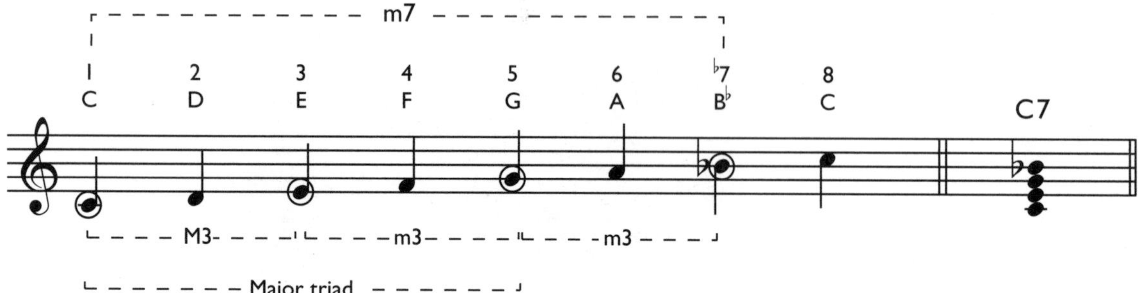

The next two types of 7 chords (like the triads they are built on) are not as common as the preceding ones. They can, however, be very effective when used at the right time.

## HALF DIMINISHED 7 CHORDS

A *half diminished 7 chord* (min7♭5) is made by placing a major 3rd above a diminished triad. This additional note is the interval of a minor 7th from the root. The intervals of this chord are 1–♭3–♭5–♭7.

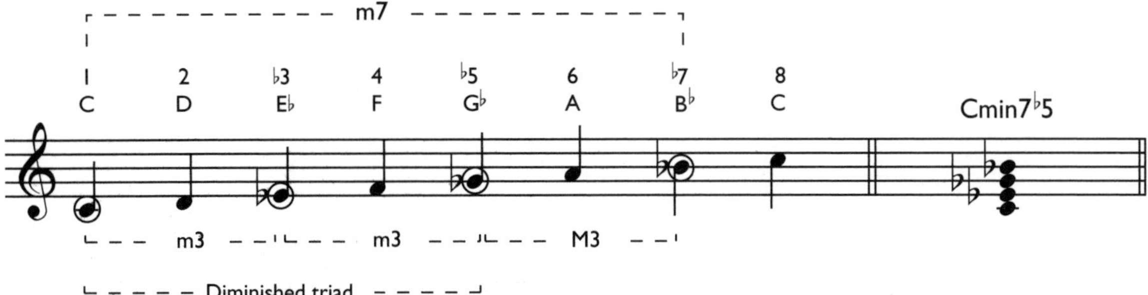


## DIMINISHED 7 CHORDS

A *diminished* 7 chord (dim7) is made by placing a minor 3rd above a diminished triad. This additional note is the interval of a diminished 7th (which is a half step lower than a minor 7th) from the root. The intervals of this chord are 1–♭3–♭5–𝄫7.*

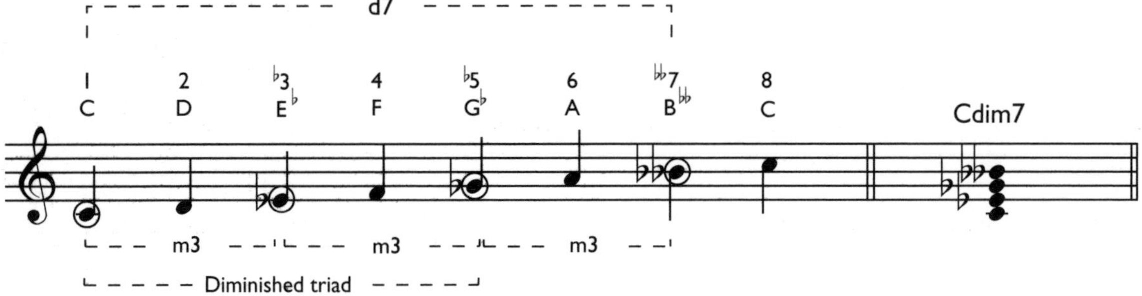


* A *double flat* 𝄫 is used to lower a note two half steps, or a whole step. This particular note (B𝄫) is the enharmonic equivalent of A.

# DIATONIC HARMONY

Now we will see how chords relate to keys. Each major scale has its unique set of notes. Each note is the root of a corresponding chord. A key is the set of all the notes and chords of a scale. These notes and chords are *diatonic,* which means they belong to the key. *Diatonic harmony* refers to the chords that belong to a particular key.

To build the chords in a major key we start with the major scale. Taking each note in the scale as a root (remember to count the root as 1), we skip a note to find the 3rd and—from the 3rd—skip another note to find the 5th. Here are the chords in the key of C:

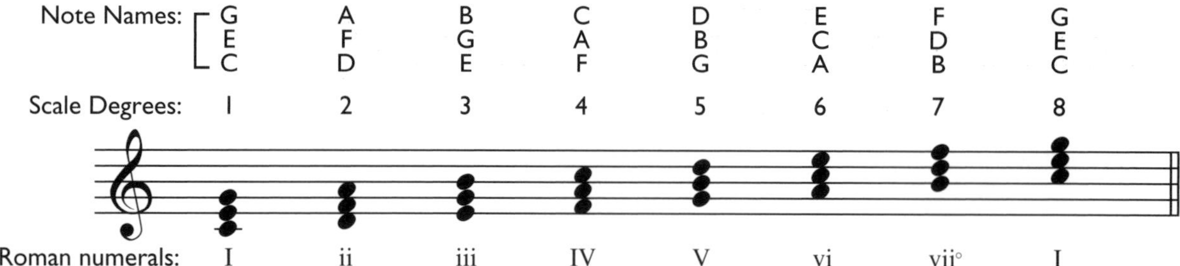


As discussed on page 20, Roman numerals are used to represent each chord. Uppercase is used for major chords (I, IV, V—the primary chords) and lowercase is used for minor and diminished chords (ii, iii, vi, vii). This sign ◦ is used to show that a chord is diminished (vii°).

The diatonic pattern of major, minor and diminished chords is the same in every major key.

| I | ii | iii | IV | V | vi | vii° | I |
|---|---|---|---|---|---|---|---|
| major | minor | minor | major | major | minor | diminished | major |

- The I, IV and V chords are always major.
- The ii, iii and vi chords are always minor.
- The vii° is always diminished.

For the sake of convenience, musicians refer to the chords of a key by their Roman numerals. You might hear a guitarist say: "It's a ii–V–I progression in the key of E." Knowing this system can help you when playing with other musicians. The primary chords are by far the most common chords in the blues. The chart to the right will help you learn these in each key. Memorize the natural note keys first, as these are the easiest.

As mentioned on page 20 (Easiest Blues Form—Analysis), in the blues we usually add the ♭7 to our I, IV and V chords to get a dominant 7 sound. The ♭7s of the I and IV chords are not diatonic notes to the major scale based on the I chord, but adding them helps to create a "bluesy" sound that is fundamental to this style.

| I | IV | V |
|---|---|---|
| C | F | G |
| G | C | D |
| D | G | A |
| A | D | E |
| E | A | B |
| B | E | F♯ |
| F♯ | B | C♯ |
| G♭ | C♭ | D♭ |
| D♭ | G♭ | A♭ |
| A♭ | D♭ | E♭ |
| E♭ | A♭ | B♭ |
| B♭ | E♭ | F |
| F | B♭ | C |

# KEY SIGNATURES

A key signature is placed after the clef on each line of music. It indicates which notes are sharp or flat—in all octaves—throughout a piece of music. The accidentals that appear in the key signature are those in the major scale of the same name. The number of sharps or flats indicates the key the music is in. The key of C Major has no sharps or flats.

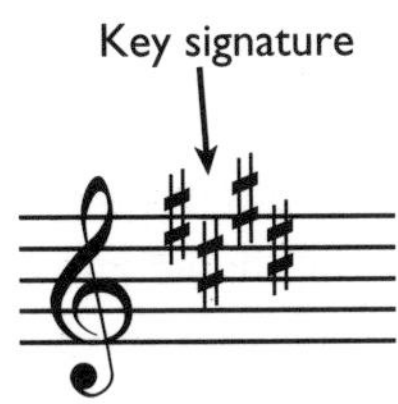


**Sharp Keys**

G MAJOR — F♯

D MAJOR — F♯ C♯

A MAJOR — F♯ C♯ G♯

E MAJOR — F♯ C♯ G♯ D♯

B MAJOR — F♯ C♯ G♯ D♯ A♯

F♯ MAJOR — F♯ C♯ G♯ D♯ A♯ E♯

C♯ MAJOR — F♯ C♯ G♯ D♯ A♯ E♯ B♯

**Flat Keys**

F MAJOR — B♭

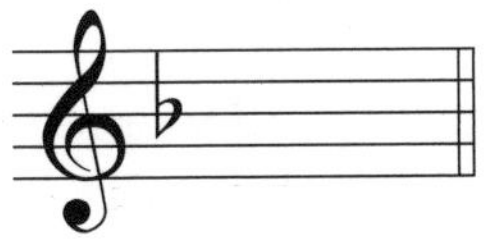

B♭ MAJOR — B♭ E♭

E♭ MAJOR — B♭ E♭ A♭

A♭ MAJOR — B♭ E♭ A♭ D♭

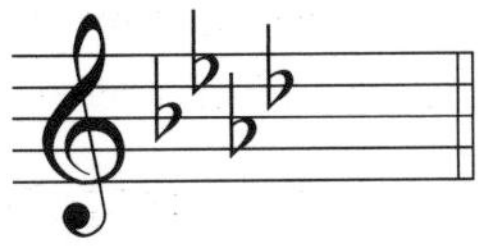

D♭ MAJOR — B♭ E♭ A♭ D♭ G♭

G♭ MAJOR — B♭ E♭ A♭ D♭ G♭ C♭

C♭ MAJOR — B♭ E♭ A♭ D♭ G♭ C♭ F♭

Knowing key signatures can help us learn songs by ear, because we come to know what notes or chords to expect in a key. Most often, the letter name of the first chord in a song will also be the name of the key.

# CHAPTER 8

# Boogie Woogie Blues Patterns

*Boogie woogie* is a blues piano style in which a pianist plays a steady eighth-note pattern with the left hand, and chords and melody with the right hand. The eighth-note pattern, which is based on the major scale, usually proceeds from the tonic, to the 3rd, to the 5th, then to the 6th and/or ♭7th. This pattern is played ascending and then descending (for example, 1–3–5–6–♭7–6–5–3, etc.). Guitarists, who have been copying this style for a long time, usually just play the left-hand part on the lower strings.

## CLOSED FORMS

Our first boogie woogie piece uses the Easiest Blues form and is in the key of G. Notice, in the TAB, it is made up entirely of fretted notes—no open strings. This sort of *closed* form allows for easy *transposition* (the changing of a piece of music to another key). By simply starting the boogie woogie pattern from a different place on the fretboard, you can transpose the pattern to a new key. After you have mastered the whole piece in G, try it in other keys by going to any other fret and playing the same patterns.

In boogie woogie style, we usually use downstrokes only. When using a fast tempo, however, you may want to alternate between downstrokes and upstrokes.

Boogie woogie sounds great when one guitarist plays the boogie woogie pattern and another strums the chords (written above the staff) at the same time. On the CD, the strums are on one channel and the boogie woogie pattern is on the other. You can use the stereo's balance control to eliminate either part and play along.

### BOOGIE WOOGIE IN G

Track 19

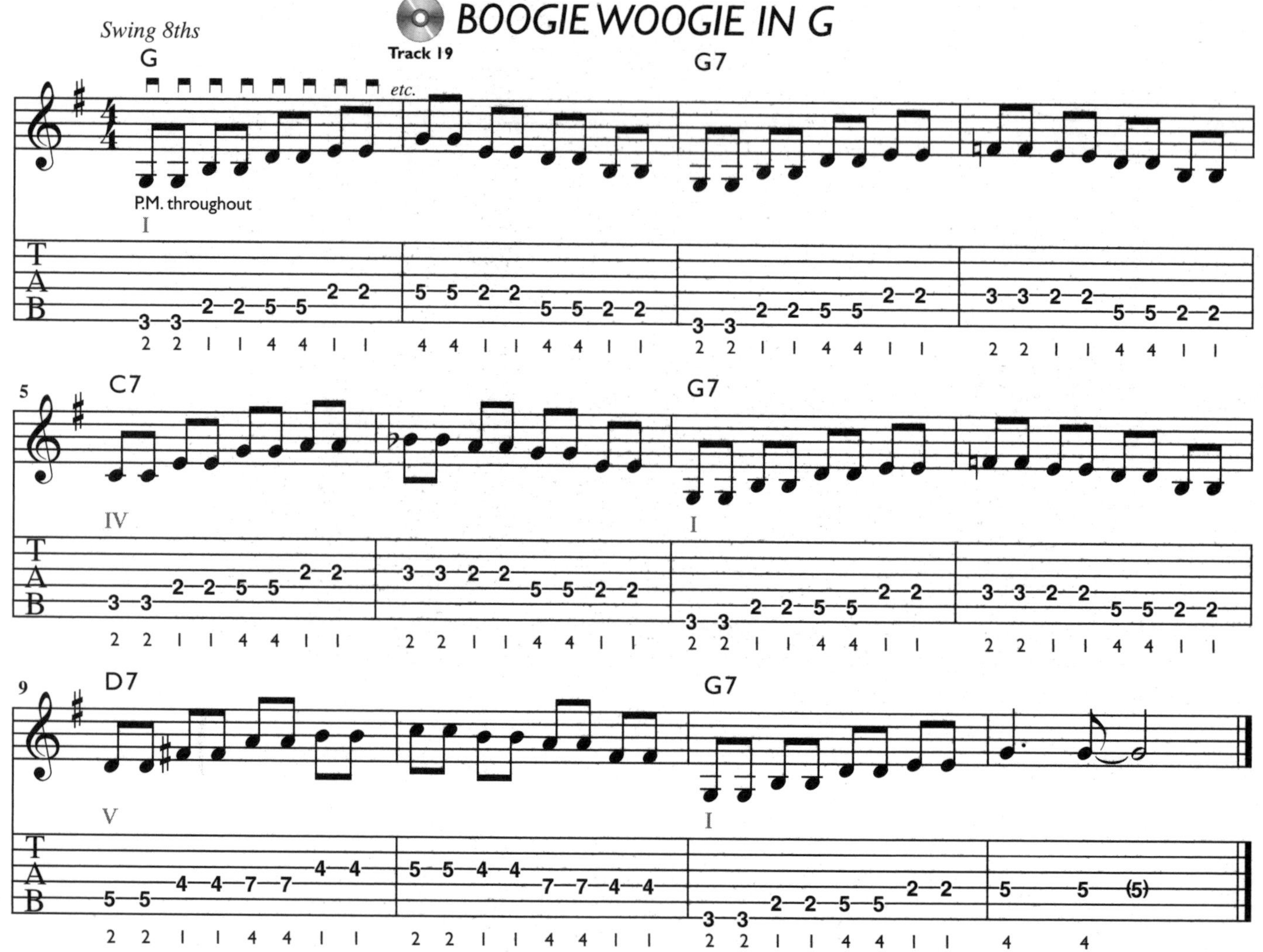

The next piece is a boogie woogie in E, probably the most common guitar key for this style. The last two bars feature a popular *turnaround.* A turnaround comes at the end of a chorus and sets the music up to go back to the beginning or to end.

Notice in this piece that measures 1–8 are in the Easiest Blues form, and measures 9–12 are in the Most Common Blues form.

## BOOGIE WOOGIE IN E

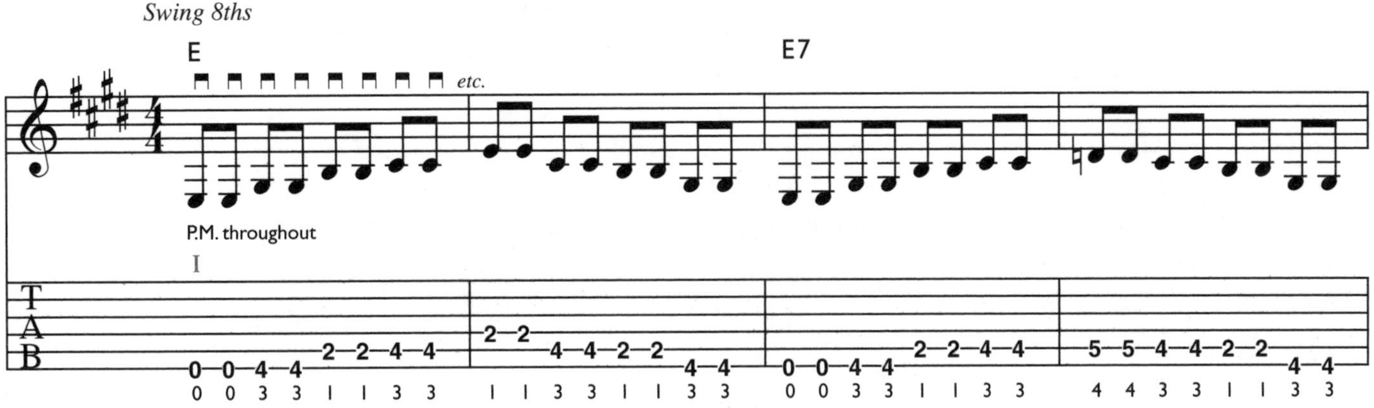


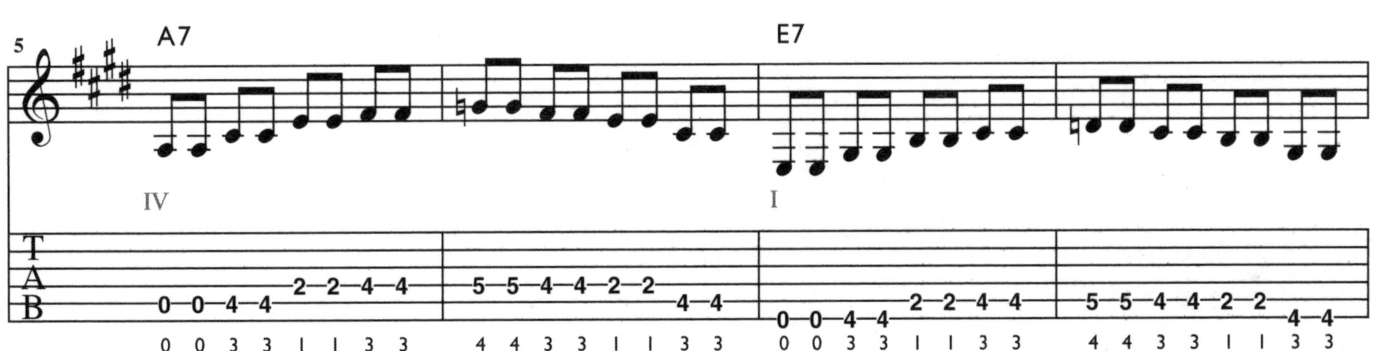


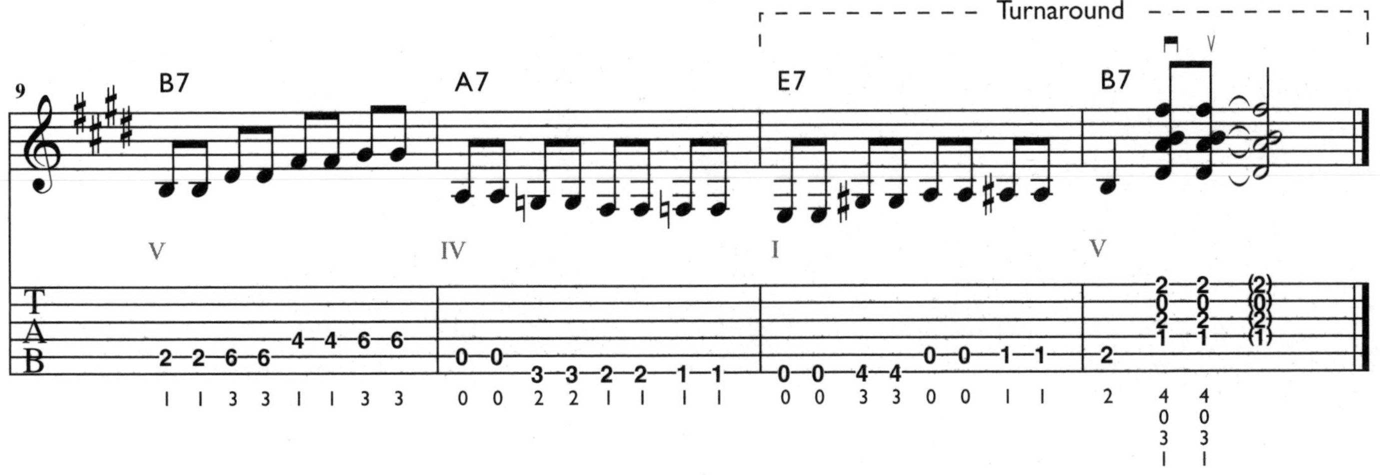

# CHAPTER 9

## Blues Strums

At a gig, a blues band may play the same progressions all night long. To keep the crowd interested, they will vary the keys and rhythms. The focus of this chapter is to teach you a variety of rhythmic patterns for blues rhythm guitar. They are exciting to play and will make your playing more interesting. We will apply these new strums to the standard 12-bar blues patterns you already know and will also introduce some new keys.

The following blues features an eighth-note strum and should be played in swing style. Remember, it is standard practice to use only downstrokes when playing two-string patterns, but when we strum full chords we usually alternate between downstrokes and upstrokes. The upstroke should be lighter than the downstroke—just hitting the first few strings, not the full chord. This gives our eighth notes the right blues bounce by accenting the first part of each beat (DA–da, DA–da, DA–da, DA–da). Use a pick at first, but later try strumming down with your thumb, and up with your index finger.

This following piece is in a new key: the key of C. The F7, the IV (see below), will probably be a new fingering for you. Practice it first and then tackle the following piece.

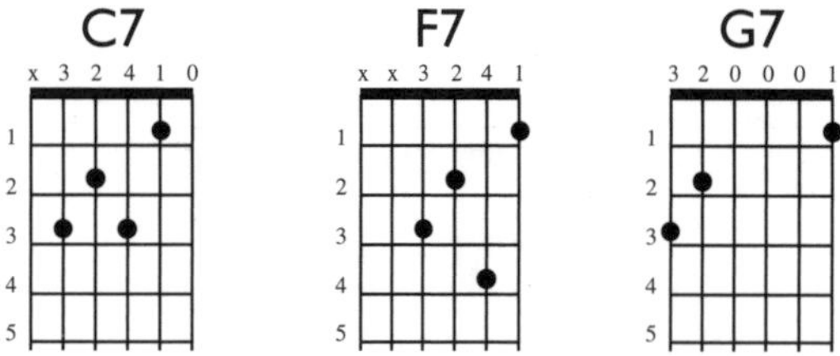

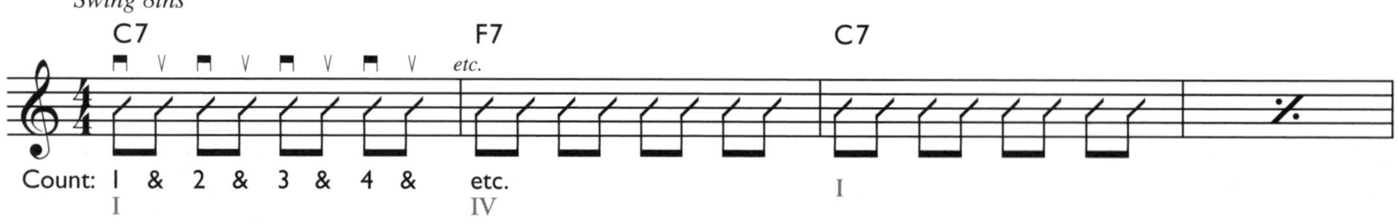


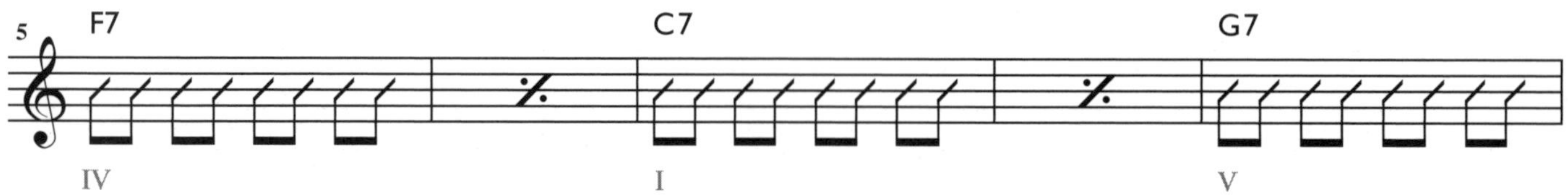


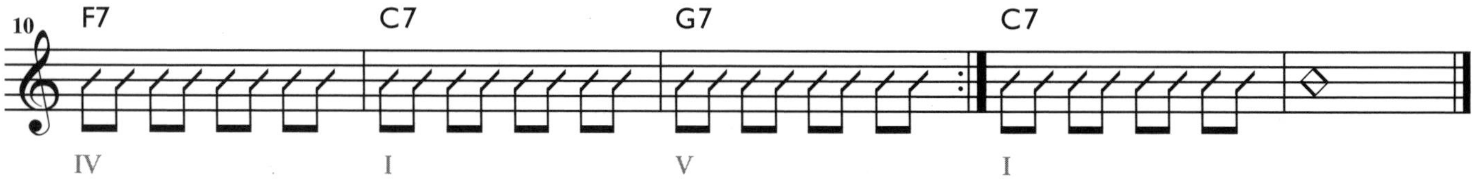

## BLUES IN $\frac{12}{8}$

In $\frac{12}{8}$ time, there are 12 beats in a bar and each eighth note gets one beat. Potentially, there can be 12 eighth notes in each bar. However, you can think of the following strum as having four beats, with three equal eighth notes in each beat. The way to count in this time is: **1**–2–3, **2**–2–3, **3**–2–3, **4**–2–3, tapping your foot down on the 1, 2, 3 and 4.

To keep this rhythm interesting, it is important to accent beats 2 and 4 (see page 21, Backbeat).

This rhythm is often used in slow blues pieces.

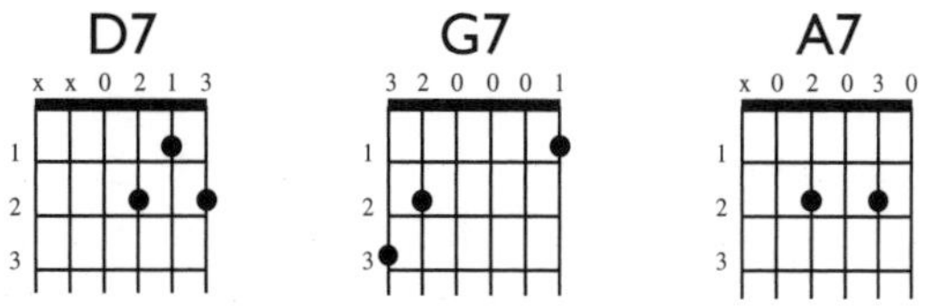

D7 (x x 0 2 1 3) G7 (3 2 0 0 0 1) A7 (x 0 2 0 3 0)

### $\frac{12}{8}$ BLUES

Track 22

> = *Accent.* Play louder.

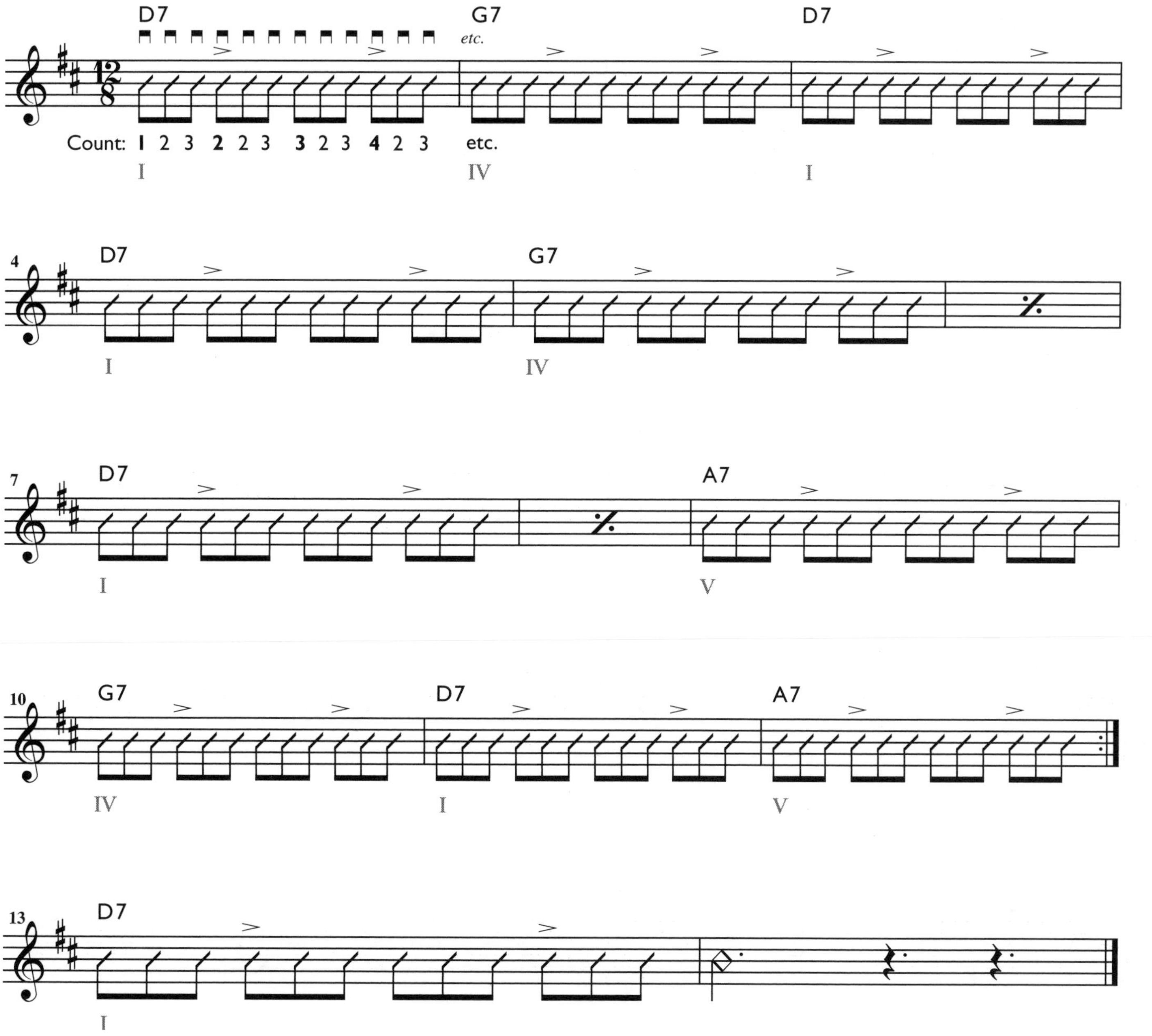

D7 | G7 *etc.* | D7

Count: **1** 2 3 **2** 2 3 **3** 2 3 **4** 2 3 etc.

I | IV | I

4 D7 | G7 | 

I | IV

7 D7 | | A7

I | V

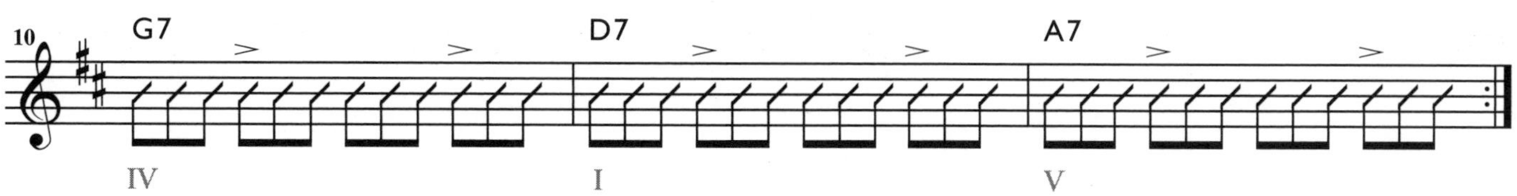


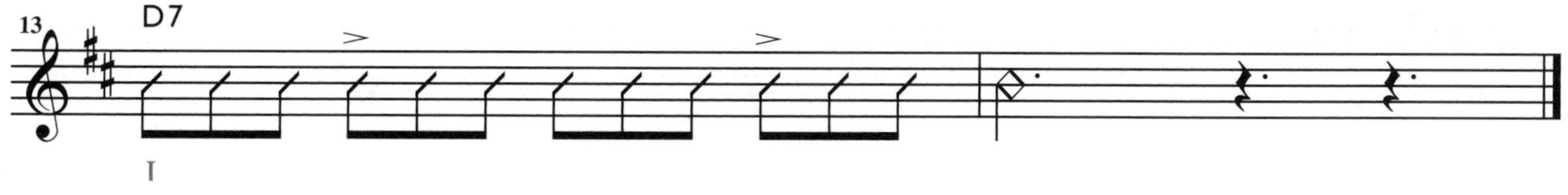

Our next example features one of the most common blues strums. It starts with a dotted quarter note on the first beat. Then there is an eighth note on the "&" of the 2nd beat which is tied to a half note. This gives us lots of "space," with only two strums in each bar. Both strums should be played with strong downstrokes. The placement of the second strum on the "&" of beat 2 creates *syncopation,* which is the shifting of emphasis from onbeats to offbeats (see page 12, Ties and Counting, for discussion of onbeats and offbeats).

When playing this rhythm, count: **1**–&, 2–**&**, 3–&,4–&, strumming down on the 1 and the "&" of beat 2. Be sure to count in swing style. Listen to the CD to make sure you are playing the rhythm correctly.

Count: 1 & 2 & 3 & 4 &

We are using a new chord form for A7. It is a partial *barre chord* (for a barre chord, one of your fingers must lie across two or more strings at the same fret). Lay your 1st finger across the 1st through 4th strings at the 2nd fret, while fretting the 3rd fret of the 1st string with your 3rd finger.

This E7 has the same fingering as D7, only moved two frets up. There is no E-note in this chord, which makes it a *rootless* chord. In blues, and especially jazz, rootless chords are not uncommon.

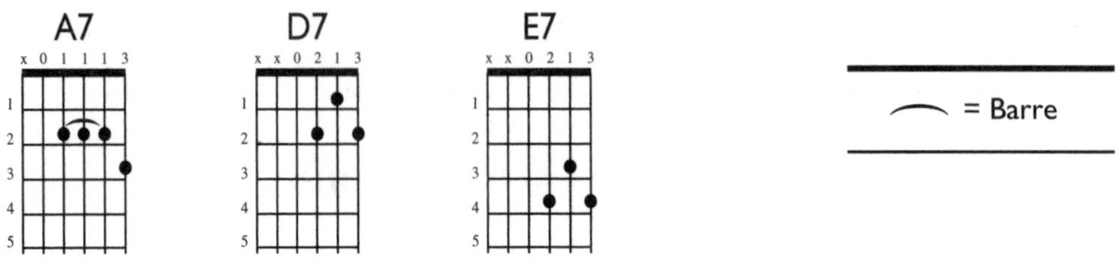


## TWO-STRUM BLUES IN A

Track 23

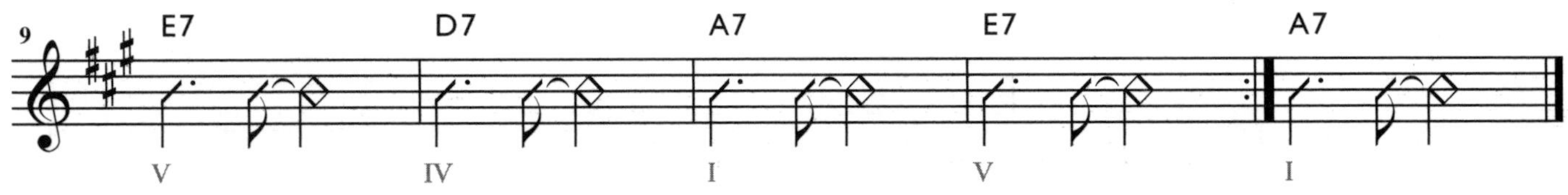

For our next piece, we've added a few more strums to the previous rhythm. Maintain the accents on beat 1 and the "&" of beat 2, strumming lighter for the rest of the measure. Be sure to strum downstrokes and upstrokes as indicated.

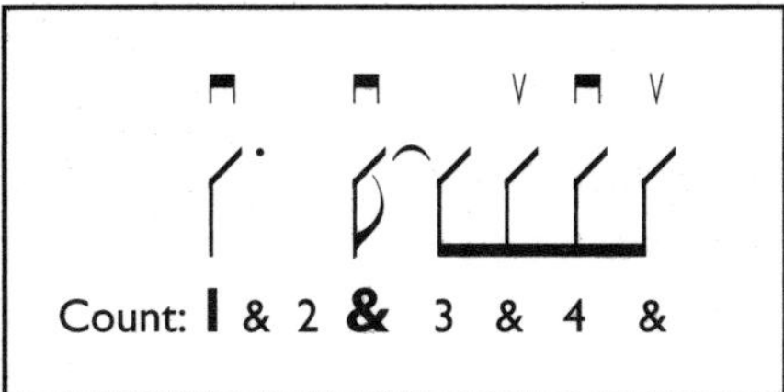


For the B7 chord, use the new A7 fingering, only two frets higher.

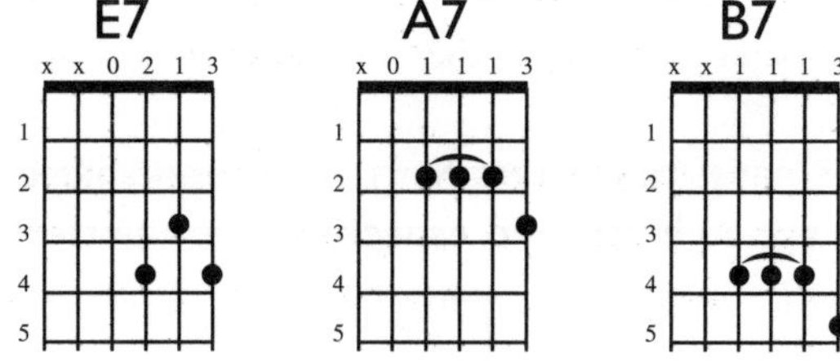

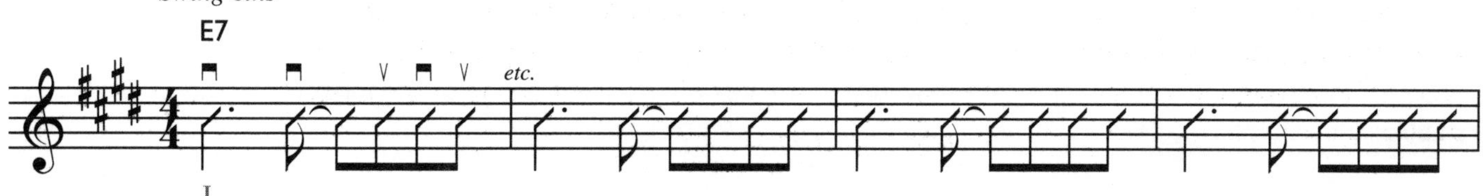


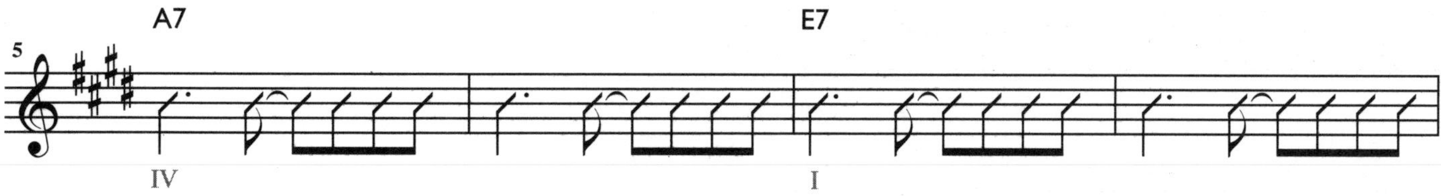


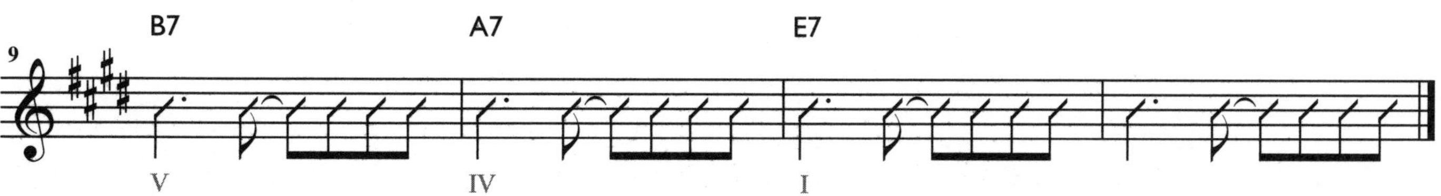

# CHAPTER 10

# Blues Soloing

*Improvising* (spontaneously creating) a good blues solo is an amazing experience. Once you know your scales and have acquired a feel for *phrasing* (the shaping of melodic lines), you'll soon be comfortable with this essential aspect of blues playing.

Learning to make up your own solos is critical. Even guitarists who play memorized solos, note-for-note, need to improvise to create their solos in the first place. Most players improvise different solos each time they play. They do, however, have a general idea of where they are "going" with their solo. Most players will also use classic *licks* in their improvisations. A lick is a short, standard phrase—part of the blues vocabulary that can be used by any player.

To be a good blues improviser, it is necessary to know the important blues scales, have a good repertoire of licks and have good phrasing. To become a real master takes a long time, but to play something simple that sounds good won't take long at all—if you practice, of course.

## THE MINOR PENTATONIC SCALE

The *minor pentatonic scale* is one of the most common scales in blues, rock and other styles. A pentatonic scale has five notes. We'll compare the minor pentatonic scale to the major scale to understand its components. We'll do this in the key of E, since it is one of the most popular blues keys.

Here are the notes in an E Major scale:

The scale degrees of every minor pentatonic scale are: 1–♭3–4–5–♭7. An E Minor Pentatonic scale has the same 1st, 4th and 5th as the E Major scale (E, A and B). If we flat the G♯, we get a G♮. G♯ is the 3rd note in the E major scale, so G♮ is considered the ♭3. Flatting the 7th, D♯, gives us a D♮. The 2nd and 6th notes from the major scale are omitted. So, the notes of an E Minor Pentatonic scale are E–G–A–B–D.

You can use the formula (1–♭3–4–5–♭7) and your knowledge of major scales to determine the notes in any minor pentatonic scale.

Here is an E Minor Pentatonic scale in open position.

8

Track 26

E Minor Pentatonic Scale
(top four strings)

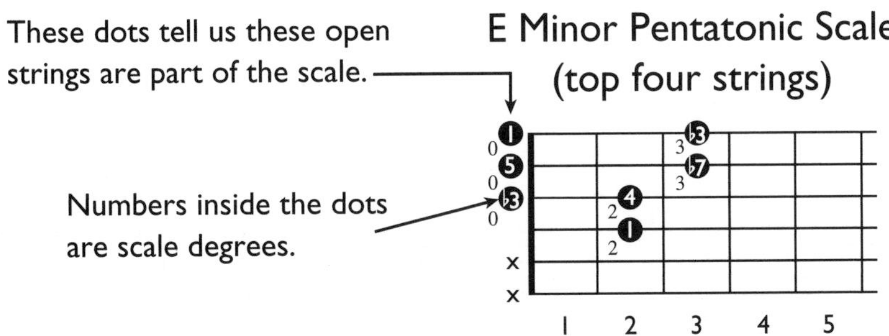


Practice all scales ascending and descending until you can play them with ease.

The following examples illustrate how parts of this scale are used to create blues phrases. Notice that they revolve around the 1, ♭3 and ♭7. These are the *target notes* (strongest or most characteristic notes) in this scale.

9

Track 27

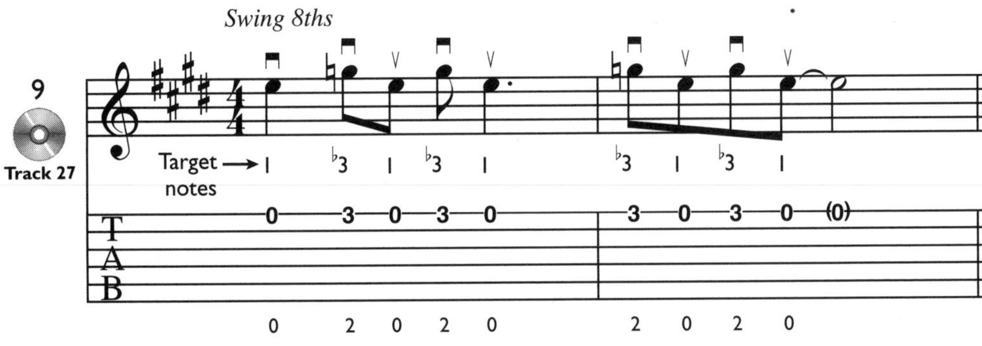


10

Track 28

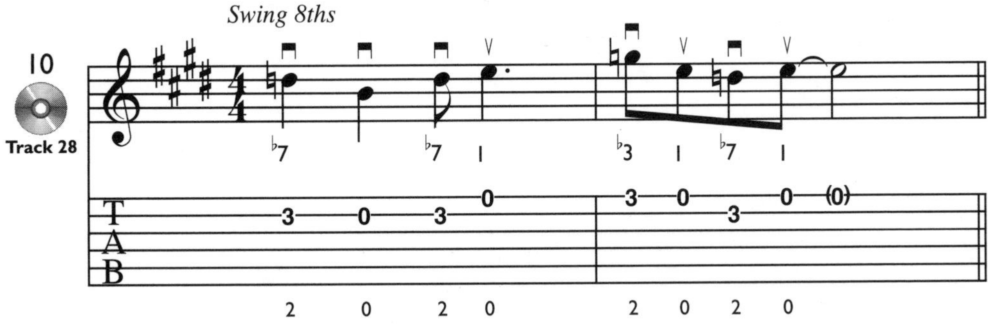

In this example, we extend the scale one note lower to a D♮ (the ♭7) on the 4th string.

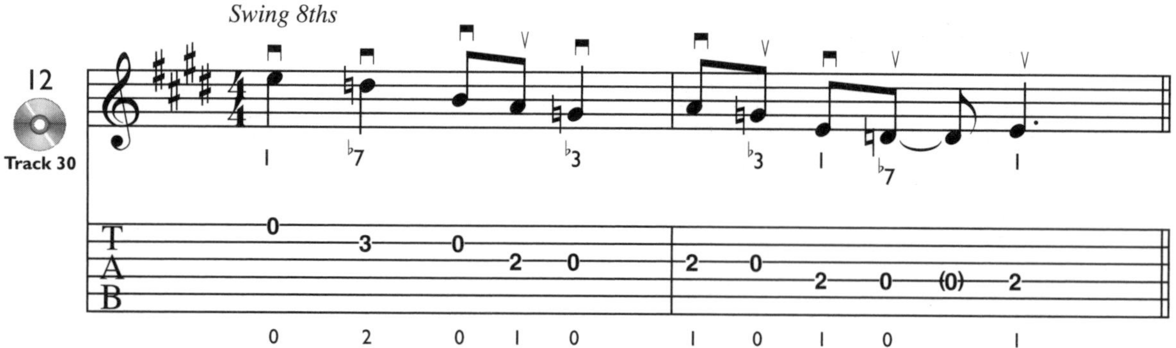


E Minor Pentatonic Scale (all six strings)

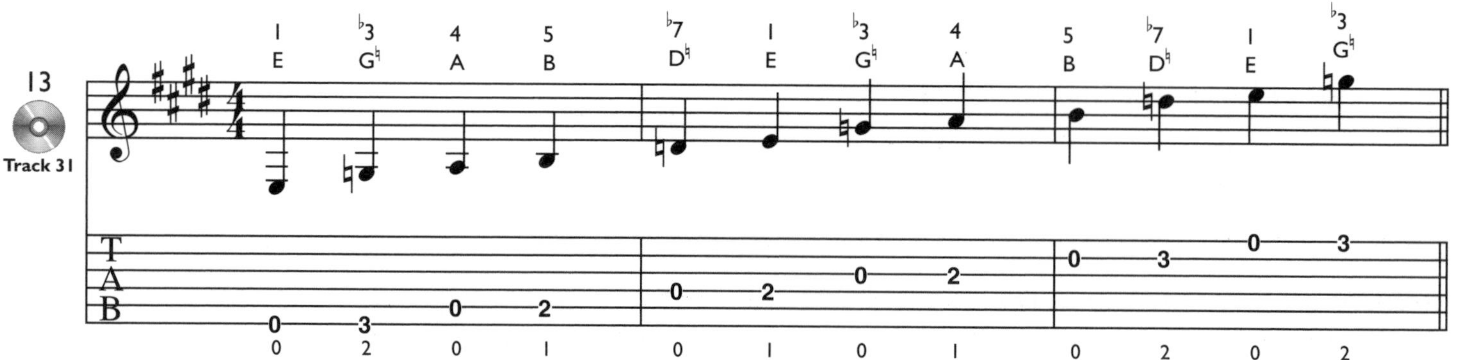


## E Minor Pentatonic Scale (all six strings)

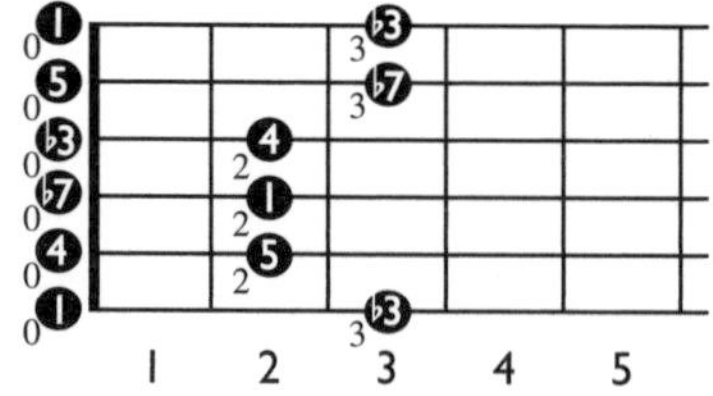

Here is a phrase using these lower notes.

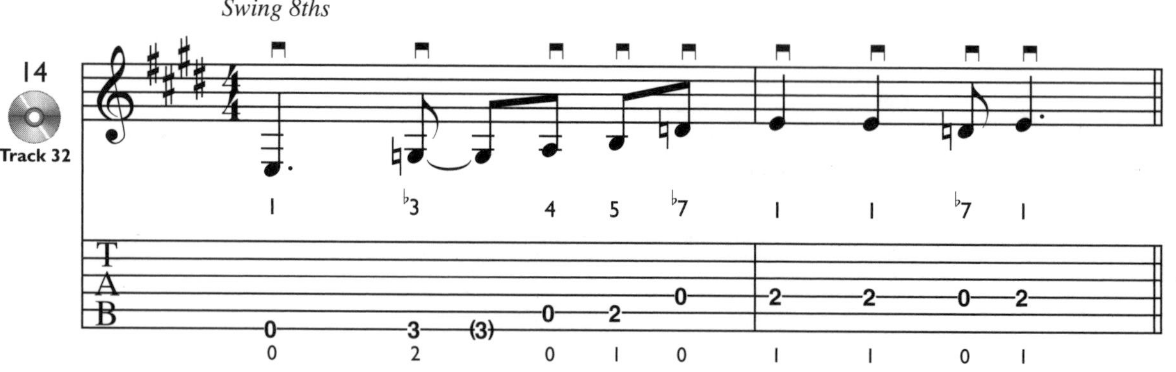

# THE MAJOR PENTATONIC SCALE

If we omit the 4 and 7 of the major scale, we create the *major pentatonic scale*. So, the scale degrees for the major pentatonic scale are 1–2–3–5–6. Like the minor pentatonic scale, it is one of the most popular scales used in the blues. It has a brighter sound than the minor pentatonic scale. Good target notes are the 1 and 3.

This fingering for the G Major Pentatonic scale has no open strings. It is a closed form (see page 42), which means it can be moved to different keys while maintaining the same fingering.

G Major Pentatonic Scale

15
Track 33

## Major Pentatonic Scale (Moveable Form)

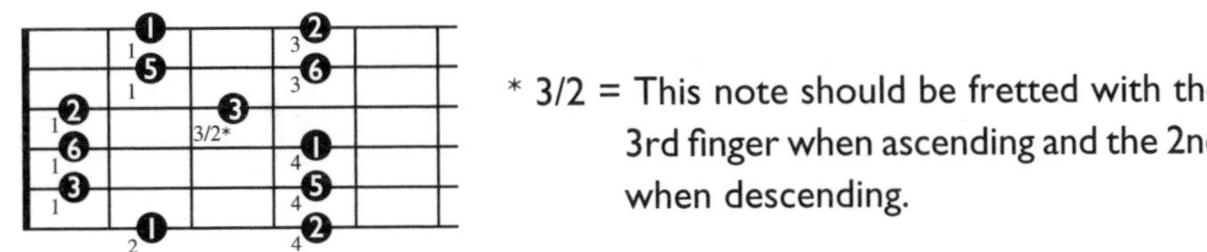


* 3/2 = This note should be fretted with the 3rd finger when ascending and the 2nd when descending.

Here are two phrases made up of common, major pentatonic scale licks.

16
Track 34

17
Track 35

# THE BLUES SCALE

There are a few widely used scales in blues, but only one is called the *blues scale*. This scale is identical to the minor pentatonic scale except for the addition of the ♭5. This is the note between the 4 and 5. We've seen that the ♭3 and ♭7 are altered notes that help to create the sound of the blues. The ♭5 goes even further in this bluesy direction. In fact, because it has such a strong and funky sound, it should be used sparingly. Normally, it is picked and then quickly resolved down to the 4—then down through the scale to the 1. It also sounds good when resolved up to the 5. The blues scale has the same target notes as the minor pentatonic scale: 1, ♭3 and ♭7. Although you don't want to overdo it, you should also target the ♭5—just enough to bring out its distinctive color.

Memorize where the ♭5s are in the following E Blues scale fingering.

E Blues Scale

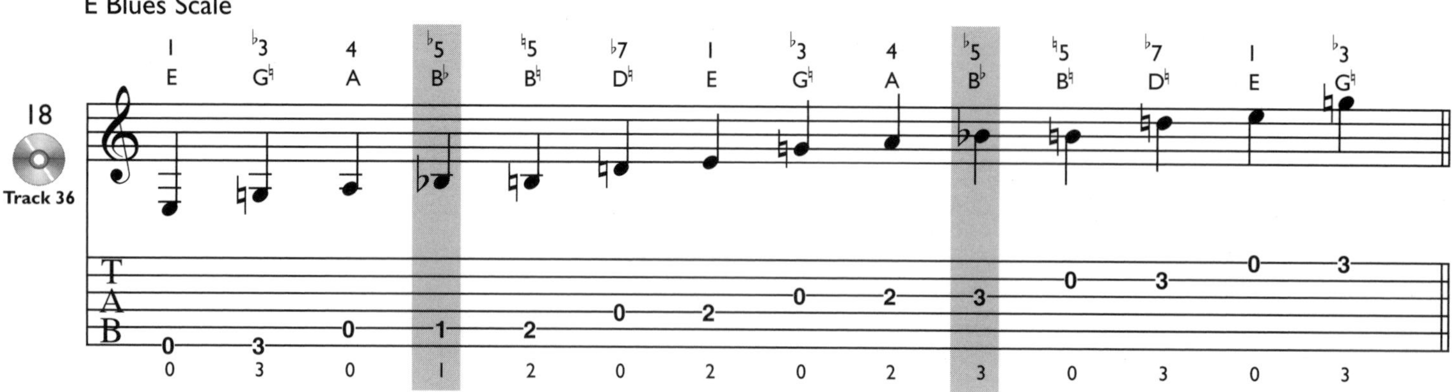


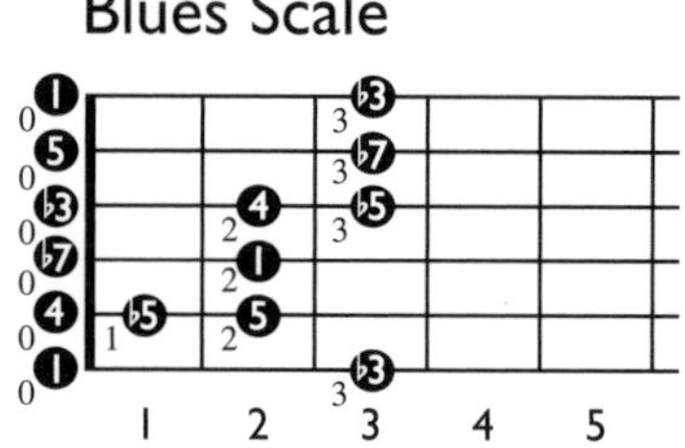


The following phrases will show you common ways to incorporate the ♭5 into your playing.

## MOVEABLE SCALE FORMS

Below are moveable versions of the minor and major pentatonic scales and the blues scale. Since they do not use open strings, they can be moved up or down the neck to any key. To do this, just move the scale to the position where the letter name of the I corresponds to the letter name of the key in which you want to play. Then start improvising, using the phrases of the preceding pages as a springboard for your own ideas.

You need to know each of the fingerings on this page; they are the most common scale forms used in the blues.

### Minor Pentatonic Scale

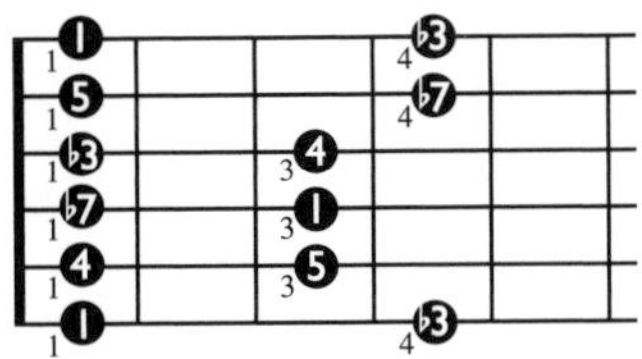

### Blues Scale

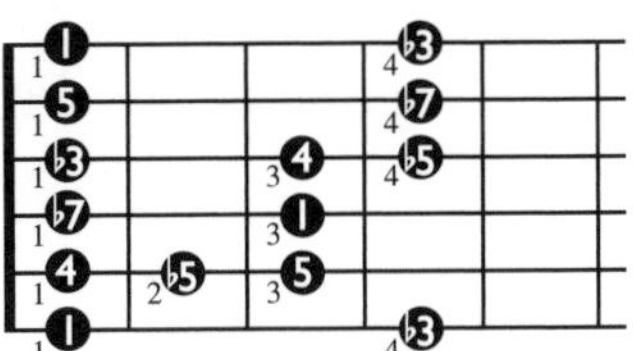

### Major Pentatonic Scale

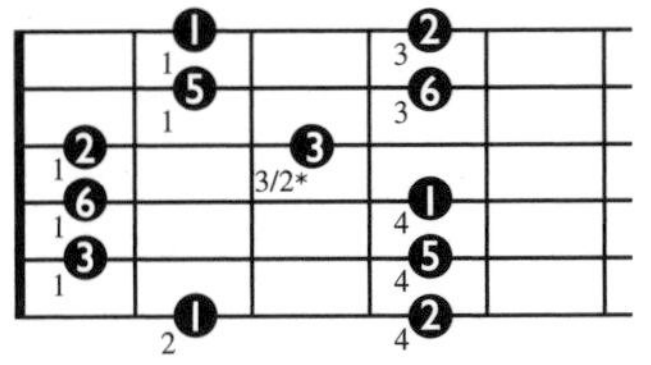

* 3rd finger ascending
2nd finger descending

### Minor Pentatonic with Upper Extension
(ascending fingering)

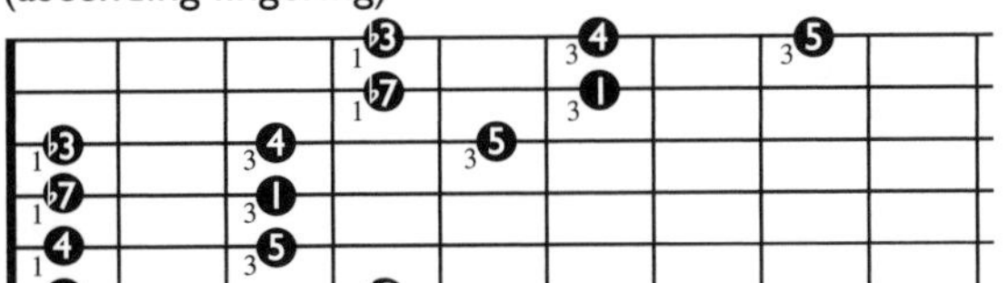

### Minor Pentatonic with Upper Extension
(descending fingering)

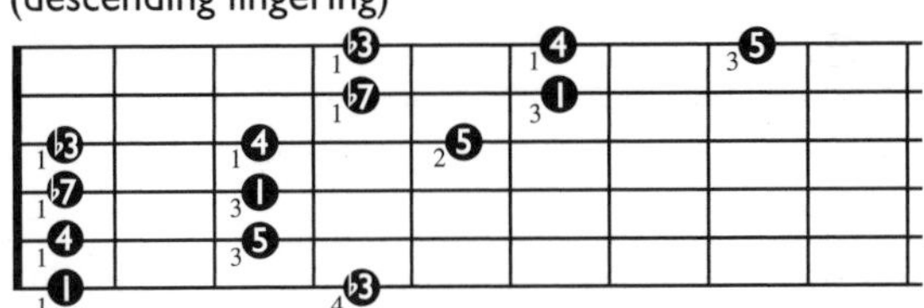

### Blues Scale
(ascending fingering)

### Blues Scale
(descending fingering)

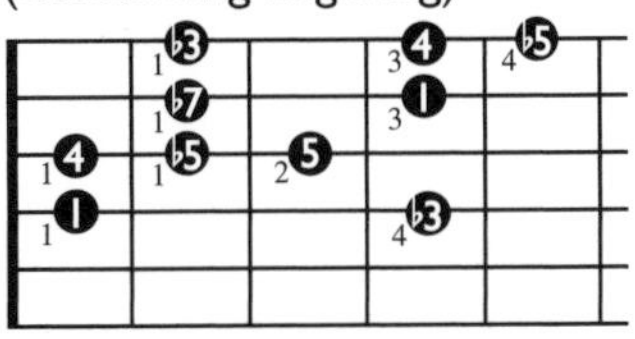

**Scale Tips**

Here are some tips to help you eventually play faster and get a fuller sound.

- Hold previously fretted notes down as you play higher notes on the same string. This sustains the lower note until the higher note is sounded.
- When moving up or down from one string to another, don't lift your fingers too soon. The finger fretting the last note on a string should stay in place as another finger moves to the next note on the next string. This creates a slight overlap and gives us continuous sound, without gaps between notes.
- Make up your own blues phrases. Try to copy the examples from this chapter using the moveable scale forms.
- Practice each scale fingering—ascending and descending—until you can play them in your sleep. Then wake up and use them when playing with other players or along with CDs.

Have fun improvising.

## PHRASING

The motto in real estate may be "location, location, location," but in blues soloing it's "phrasing, phrasing, phrasing." Phrasing is how we put notes together to make musical statements. As you play more and more, your phrasing will improve. Listen to the phrasing of great blues artists like B.B. King. Stay focused when you solo. You really need to be "in the moment" to make interesting musical choices with the notes and rhythms you play.

### PHRASING TIPS

- **Do not play too many notes.**
  You don't need to use every note in the scale for every solo. Develop licks that you can play on one or two strings. You can make a great solo with only one or two notes if you use cool rhythms. Someone once said that if you play a lot of notes, it will sound like you're looking for the right one.

- **Phrases should revolve around target notes.**
  Remember that each scale has target notes that are used more than other notes in the scale. The I, or tonic, is the most important note in any key; it's a good beginning and ending note for phrases. The ♭3, ♭5 and ♭7 are colorful notes that help to create the blues sound. In a major key, target notes are the I and ♮3. Be sure, though, not to start and end each phrase with one of these notes. Use others for interest and variety. The tonic is *stable,* which means it does not need to be resolved to any other note, but ending on another note can create suspense and "leave you hanging."

- **Repeat melodic fragments and full phrases.**
  You don't need a lot of different ideas for a solo. Repetition allows the listener to more fully absorb good phrases or statements. To add variety, try repeating phrases, but on different beats in a measure.

- **Add color and excitement by regularly using expressive techniques** such as hammer-ons, pull-offs, slides, bends and vibrato (all covered in the next chapter, Left-Hand Techniques, page 55).

- **Create "space" in your solos.**
  Beginners often try to fill every moment with notes, but this will sound too busy. Add space between your phrases to let the audience absorb the music. A long pause can create tension and will add more excitement to the next phrase.

- **Add interest by varying your rhythms.**
  Eighth notes are the most common rhythmic value in blues soloing, but use longer and shorter values for variety.

- **Listen to recorded solos that move you and imitate them.**
  Try to copy the licks and phrases, or at least copy the rhythms to create your own musical statements.

- **Express yourself.**
  Focus on the emotion you want to convey and put it into your playing.

# CHAPTER 11

# Left-Hand Techniques

In this chapter, we will cover techniques that are absolutely vital for blues players. All of them, except one, are *legato* techniques. On the guitar, they are produced when we pick one note and sound other notes with our left hand. Practice all of the examples until they become comfortable. Then try to incorporate them into your soloing.

## HAMMER-ONS

To play a *hammer-on,* pick one note and sound the next note on the same string by "hammering-on" with a left-hand finger. The second note is not picked. To do this effectively, you need to bring your left-hand finger down cleanly on the fret, just behind the fret wire. Think of tapping the note with your left-hand finger, rather than just fretting it. In a good hammer-on, each note will be equal in volume. A curved line ⌒ called a slur, connecting one note to a higher note, indicates a hammer-on.

The following example shows the E Minor Pentatonic scale played with hammer-ons.

H = Hammer-on

This phrase starts with a common hammer-on lick.

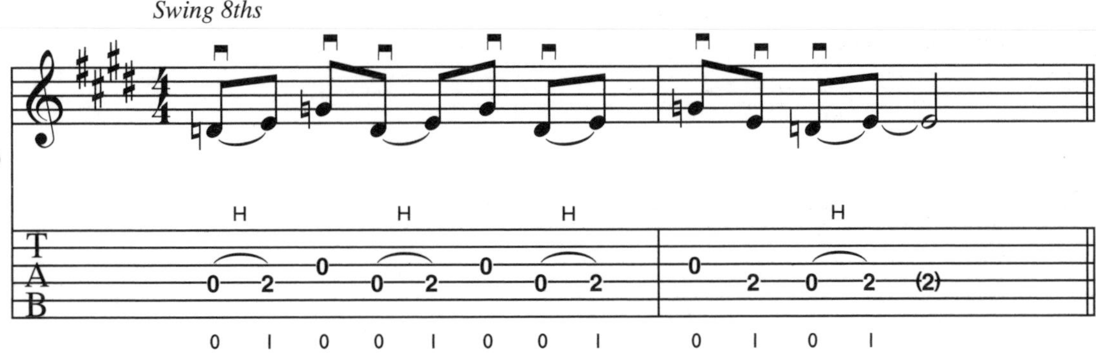

## PULL-OFFS

A slur connecting one note to a lower note indicates a *pull-off*. This technique is accomplished by picking a fretted note, then "pulling-off" with the left-hand finger that is fretting the note. This activates a lower note on the same string. The second note can be open or fretted. If it's a fretted note, your finger must be in place ahead of time, before the pull-off is set into motion. With a little practice, both notes should be equal in volume. Keep in mind that you cannot pull-off from an open string.

A more appropriate name for pull-offs would be "pull-downs," because a downward motion (toward the floor) is needed for a strong second note. As a demonstration of this, put a left-hand finger on a note and, without picking the string, lift your finger horizontally off the string. You'll notice that a very quiet sound is produced. Now fret the same note again. Do not pick the string, but move your finger downward, staying in contact with the fretboard. Flick the string as your finger moves down. The lower note should ring clearly and your finger should come to rest against the next string (if you pull-off on the 1st string, your finger would wind up just off the neck). By doing this, you will have two strong notes. At first, you may sound unwanted open strings when you pull-off. If this occurs, practice muting the open strings with the sides of your left-hand fingers or right-hand palm.

Here is a descending E Minor Pentatonic scale played with pull-offs.

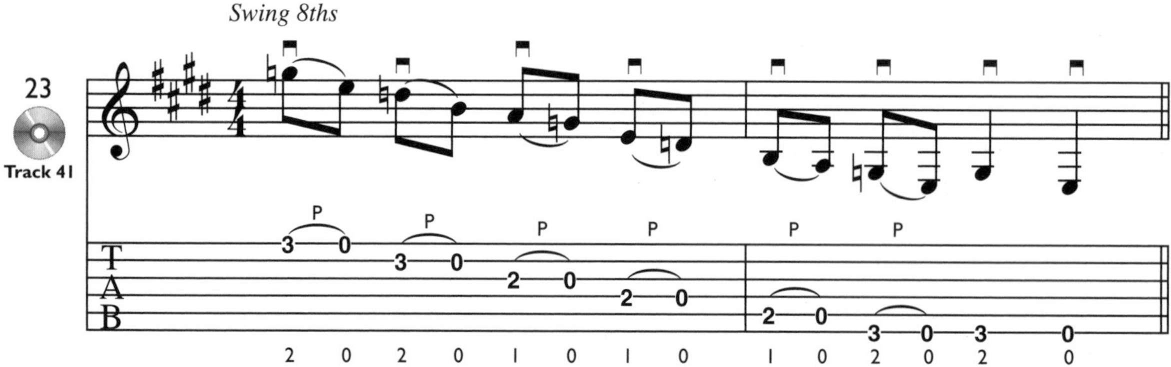


P = Pull-off

The pull-offs in this phrase are common in blues soloing.

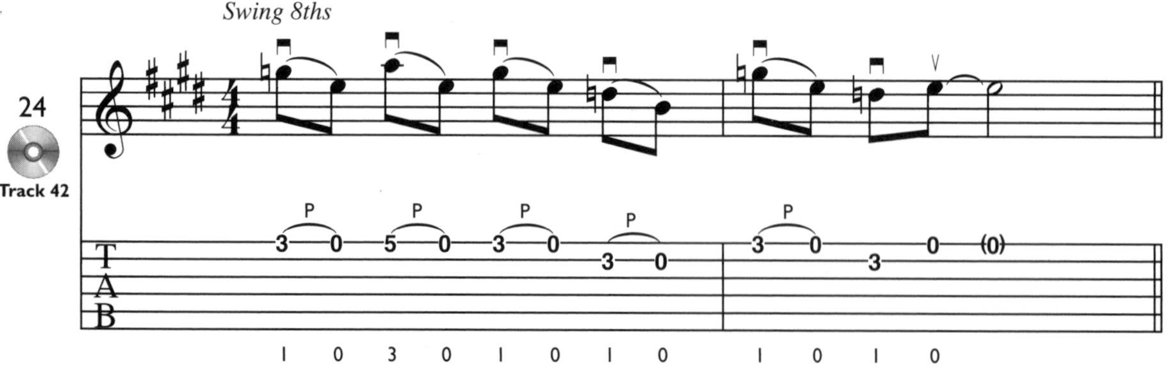

# BENDING

The *bend* is one of the most expressive techniques in the blues and it is often used to imitate the phrasing of the human voice. To bend, play a fretted note and bend—or push—the string to get the pitch of another note.

When bending, we need to have a "destination" note in mind. We push the string until we get the sound of a second note. This second note is almost always another note in the scale; we bend from one scale-note to the pitch of another. At first, your destination note may sound out of tune; you may be bending too far or not far enough to get an accurate pitch on the second note. When practicing bends, play your destination note first and get the sound of it in your mind. Then practice bending to that sound. You can also use an electronic tuner to help you practice bending to the correct note.

In acoustic blues, we use half-step and whole-step bends. Bending works best on the first two strings because they are the thinnest. It is also easier to bend in the middle of the neck, where the strings are looser and have more "give." In TAB and standard music notation, bends are indicated by a curved arrow. The number above the arrow tells us if it is a half- or whole-step bend.

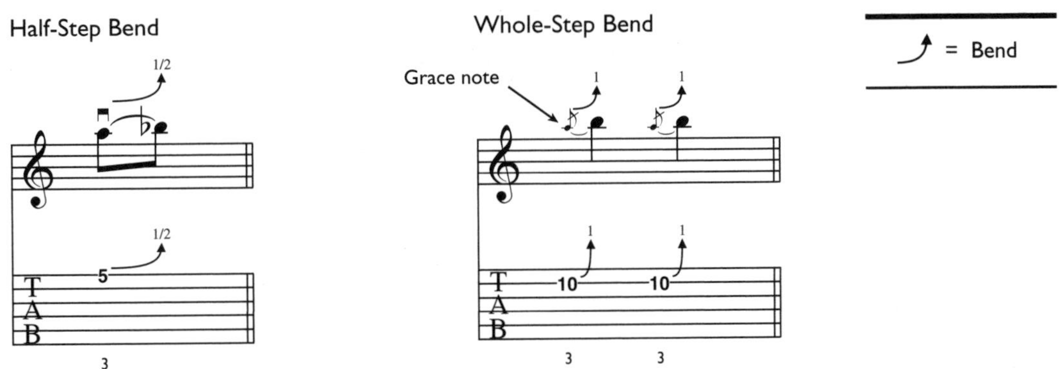


Aside from the distance of the bend (half or whole step), there other differences between bends. In one case, we let the first note ring for a full rhythmic value (see illustration for half-step bend above). In another case, we pick a note and bend so fast that we do not let the first note ring out. This is actually a way of playing the second note; it is an *embellishment.* In this type of bend, the first note is called a *grace note.* In standard music notation, a grace note is written as a tiny eighth-note, but in TAB, it is written the same way as any other note. So if you're reading the tablature, make sure you look at the standard music notation to see if a note is a grace note or not.

Learn to bend notes with more than one finger. For example, when bending the 5th fret on the 1st string, use your 3rd finger on the 5th fret, but also place your 2nd finger on the 4th fret, and your 1st finger on the 3rd fret. This is the secret to better bending. It gives you more strength and control. Sometimes, though, we *do* bend with the 1st finger alone—so this also must be practiced. In fact, it's a good idea to practice bending with every finger. For most bends, you will be pushing the string up toward the ceiling, but for those on the 5th and 6th strings, you will pull the string down toward the floor.

Learn the common bend-notes in each scale: the 4 and $\flat 7$ in the minor pentatonic and blues scales, and the 2 in the major pentatonic scale.

Here are a couple of simple phrases that use bends.

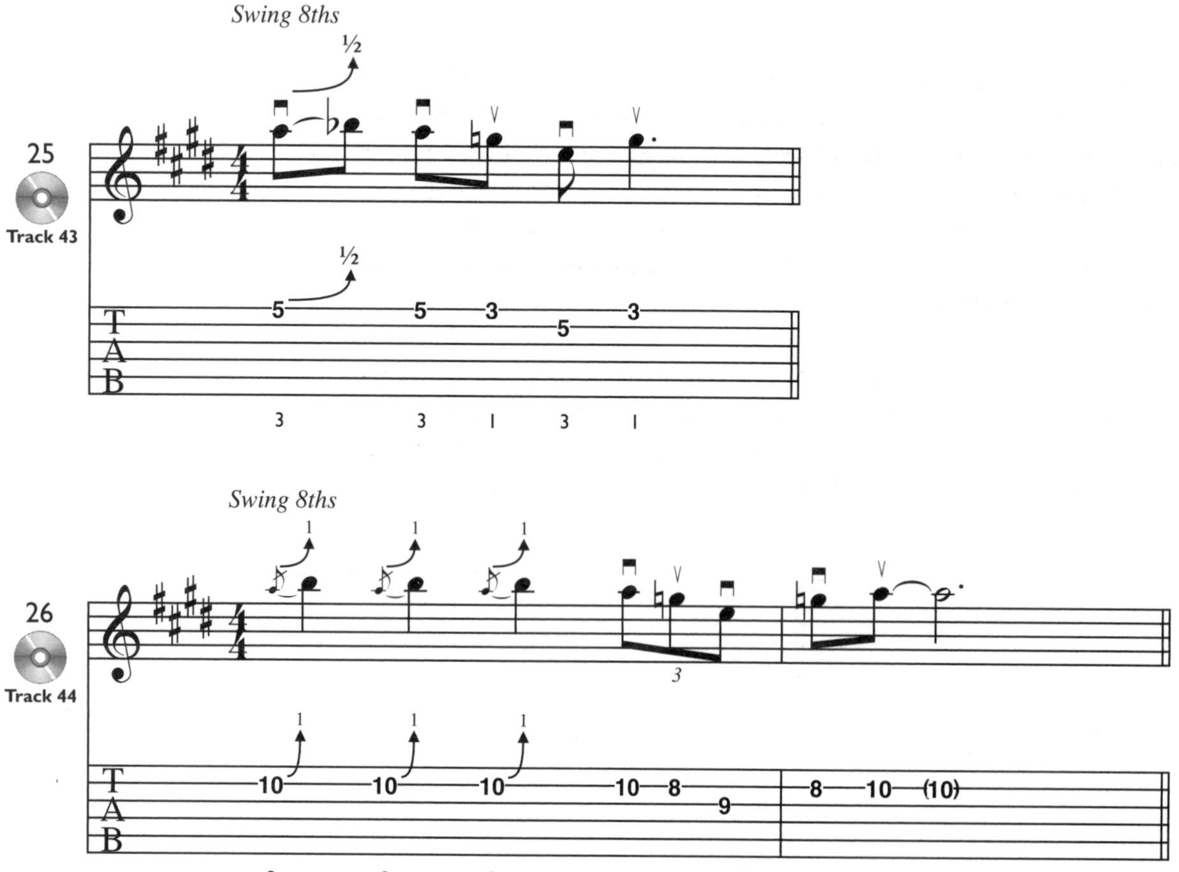


## PRE-BENDS AND REVERSE BENDS

This next example demonstrates the *reverse bend.* Here, we *pre-bend* a note before striking it. Bend first, then pick the string and release the bend. It's a great technique, but be sure to keep the finger pressure on the note or it will die out.

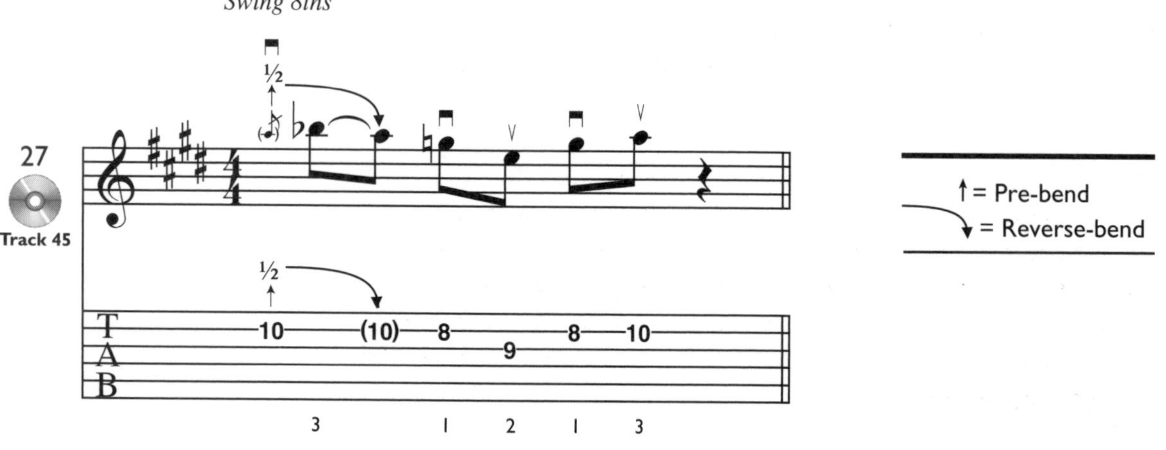

# SLIDES

A *slide* is accomplished by picking one fretted note and, keeping finger pressure on the string, sliding to a second note on the same string. Slides can be played ascending and descending.

There are three kinds of slides: *measured, grace-note* and *unspecified.* In a measured slide, the first note rings for a full rhythmic value. In a grace-note slide, we pick a note and quickly slide to the next, not allowing the first to sustain at all. In this type of slide, the first note is a grace note. In an unspecified slide, in which a starting location is not given, you can usually start a whole or half step below the destination note.

A slide is indicated by a straight line between two notes.

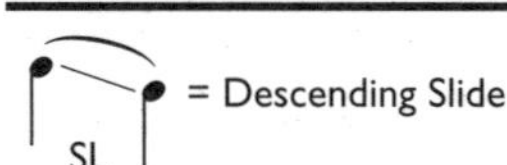


Measured Slide

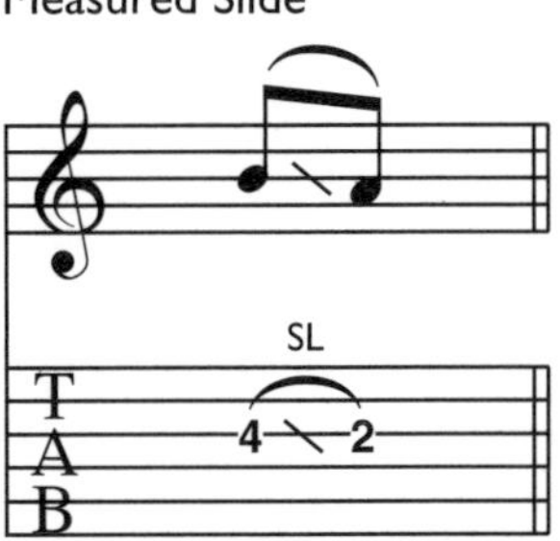


Grace-Note Slide

Unspecified Slide

The following phrase uses grace-note slides on the upper three strings.

Below, we are sliding to notes on the 2nd string while playing the open 1st string. In the first bar, the E on the 2nd string and the E on the 1st string are *unisons.* In this example, we are using unspecified slides. In the 1st measure, you can start from the 3rd fret and slide up to the 5th fret. However, in the next measure, it would make sense to start from the 5th fret (because you are already there) and slide up to the 8th fret. Experiment. See what sounds best to you.

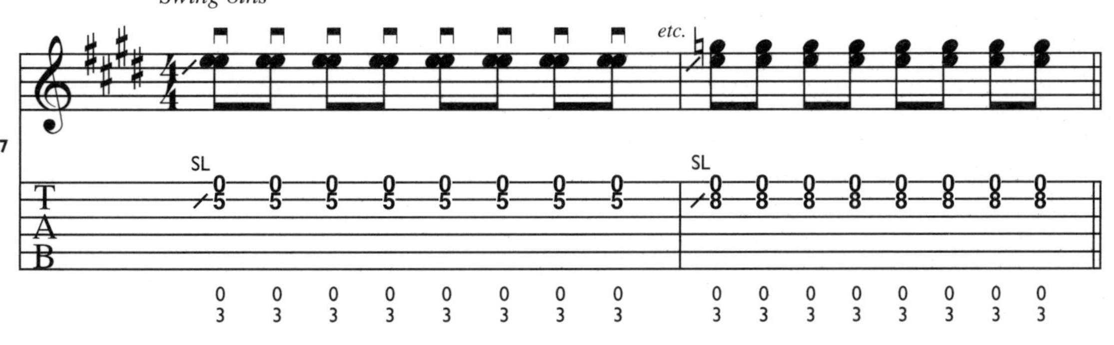

# VIBRATO

This left-hand technique is *not* a slur. *Vibrato* is a series of quick, tiny bends and is often used on the last notes and other longer notes in blues phrases. Listen to all of the great blues players and singers and you will hear a distinct fluctuation of pitch on their ending notes. This adds liveliness and sustain to a note.

To use this technique, play a fretted note anywhere on the neck. Pretend to "itch" the note after you pick it, by moving your finger slightly up and down. Be sure to keep pressure on the note and you will hear the pitch fluctuate. Try to keep this fluctuation even. Vibrato can be fast or slow depending upon the speed of your movement. It can also be wide or narrow depending on how far the finger moves from its starting spot. Most players shoot for a narrow vibrato of moderate speed. Listen to your favorite artists to check out their approach. Learn to automatically apply vibrato to your longer notes.

Vibrato is indicated by a wavy line.

| ~~~ = Vibrato |
|---|

Try the following examples using vibrato.

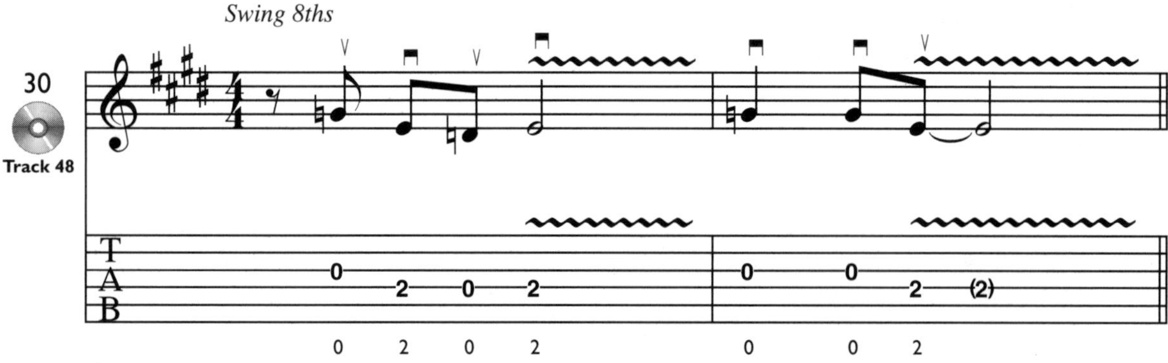


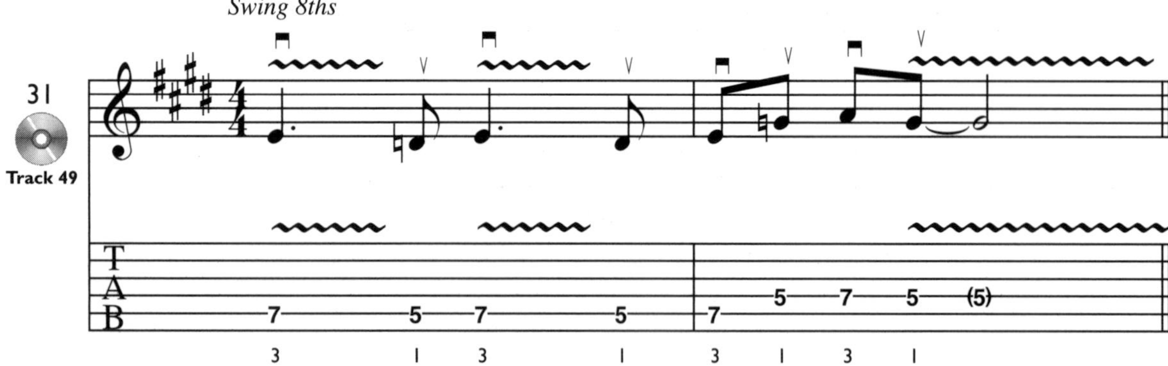

# COMBINING TECHNIQUES

A good player will combine the techniques covered in this chapter, using some more than others. This is part of what makes their individual style.

The following phrases combine the techniques covered in this chapter.

Watch out for the consecutive pull-offs in the 1st measure. Your 1st finger must be in place on the 3rd fret before you start the pull-off on the 5th fret.

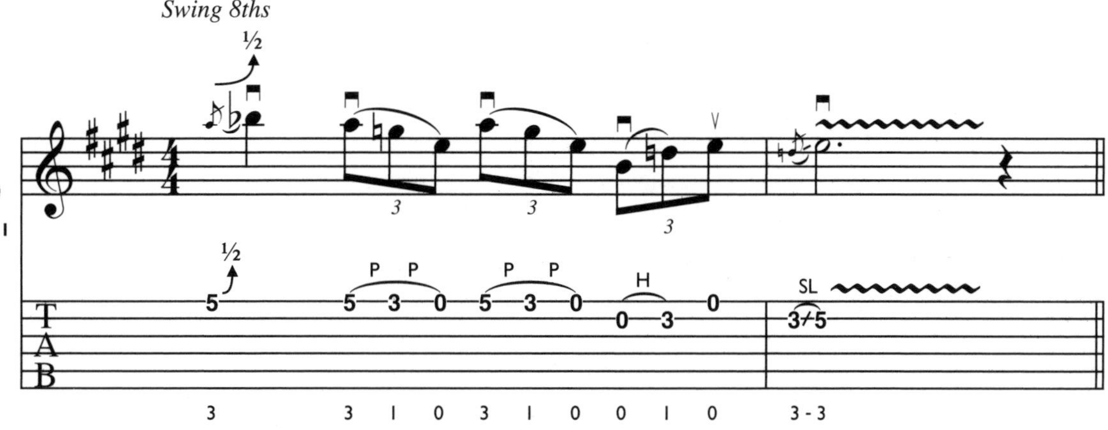

# CHAPTER 12

# More Blues Strums and Right-Hand Patterns

To the right are the chords you will need in the following examples.

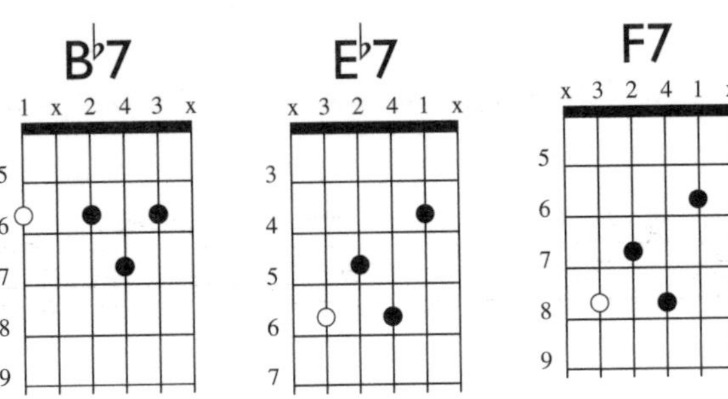


The voicing for B♭7 is a new one for you. It's very common and has a great sound. E♭7 and F7 have the same shape as the C7 chord we learned on page 24, but here we move it up the neck to other positions. There are no open strings in these chords; this makes them *closed voicings*. Be sure to mute the strings that are not part of these chords. Do this by touching them with the sides of the fingers that are fretting notes, or by using other parts of your left hand. This is tricky at first, but you'll get used to it in time. In this book, hollow dots indicate the roots of all chords with closed voicings.

The first new strum we will try is similar to the one we learned on page 46. In both strums, we strike the strings in the same rhythm, but there is an important difference. In the earlier strum we extended the note values with ties. Here we will cut each strum short with rests.

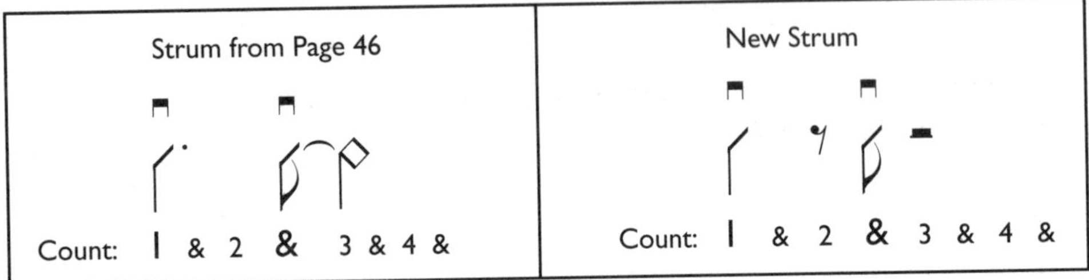


We want a percussive and choppy sound. This style is easy to achieve with closed voicings. After each strum, immediately lift your left-hand fingers—just slightly—to stop the strings from vibrating. Do not lift off the strings completely—just enough to stop the chord from ringing. With open string chords, this is more difficult. The chord must be silenced by quickly touching the strings with the side of your picking hand.

The key of B♭ is often used in jazz-blues, or when playing with sax or brass players.

## B♭ BLUES

Track 52

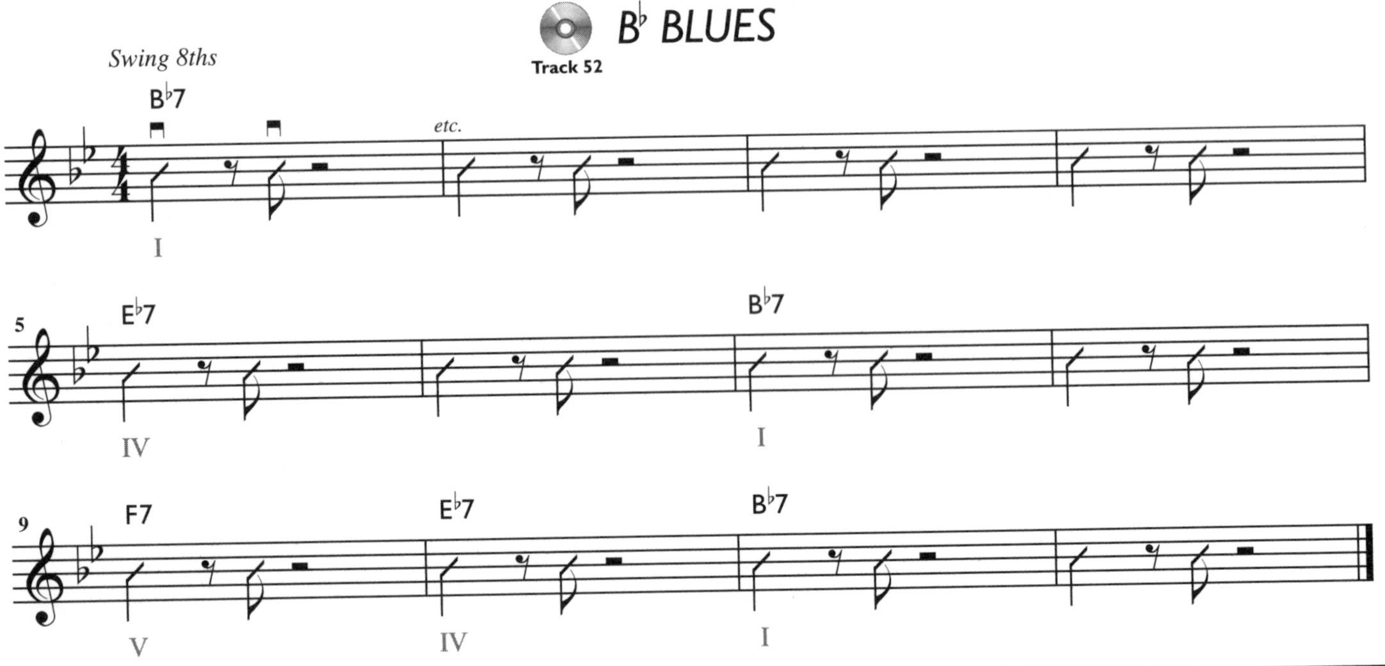

# ARPEGGIOS

*Arpeggios* are the notes of a chord played one at a time. This produces a lighter texture than strumming full chords. Arpeggios can be played using any combination of strings, but the string pattern for our example is 4th–3rd–2nd–1st–2nd–3rd, etc.

You can use a pick or you can try it fingerstyle. When playing fingerstyle, use your thumb for the 4th string, your index finger for the 3rd string, your middle finger for the 2nd string and your ring finger on the 1st string.

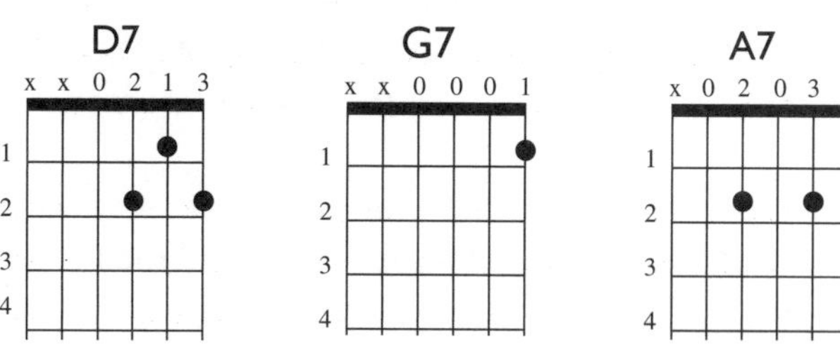

Track 53

## ARPEGGION BLUES

D7 G7 D7

I IV I

etc.

D7 G7

I IV

D7 A7

I V

G7 D7 A7 D7

IV I V I

# THE SIXTEENTH-NOTE STRUM

Our next rhythm is made up entirely of sixteenth notes. Remember, the duration of a sixteenth note is a quarter of a beat. They are counted: "1–e–&–ah, 2–e–&–ah, etc."

In our next piece, there will be four sixteenth notes for every beat in each measure. If we were to play a measure of eighth notes, and then a measure of sixteenth notes at the same tempo, the sixteenth notes would sound twice as fast as the eighth notes.

Strums like this are more common in funk guitar, but blues can be funky too. Keep your right hand and arm loose and steady. Be sure to accent the first sixteenth note of each set of four. Rhythms like this are often played with *9 chords*. The scale degrees that make up a 9 chord are 1–3–5–♭7–9. In this tune, the IV and V are 9 chords.

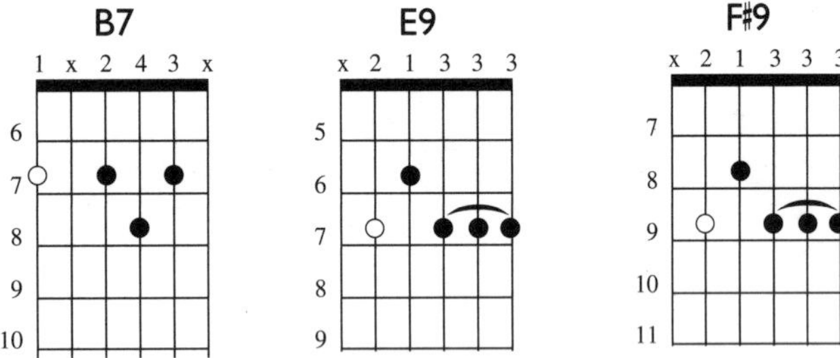

## *FUNKY BLUES IN B*

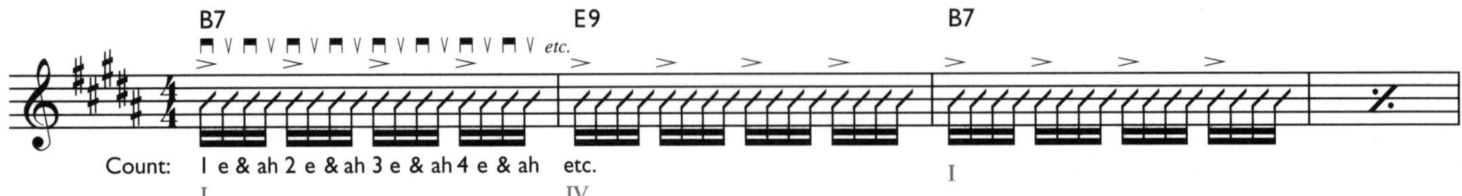


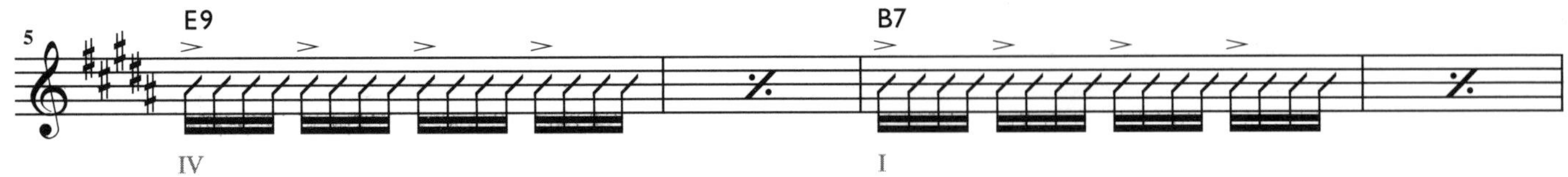


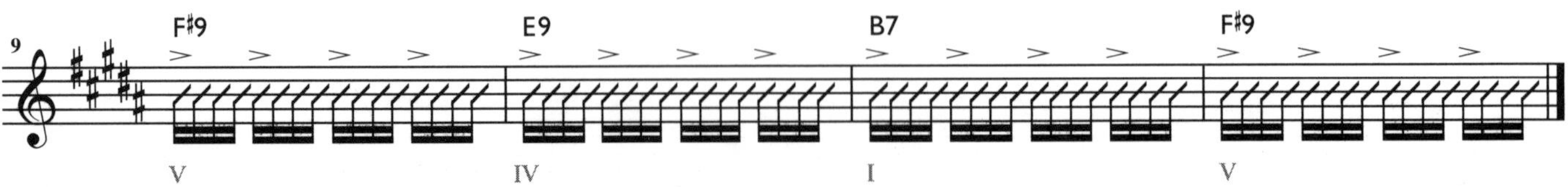

## UPBEAT STRUM

At fast tempos, players will sometimes use a strum that consists of only upstrokes played on the offbeats (&s). These are usually played with a short, choppy feel. On the acoustic guitar, it sounds great if you tap the strings with your right hand on the onbeats. The sound you are looking for is that of your hand lightly hitting the body, along with the metallic sound the strings make as they tap the frets on the neck. It's a great percussive sound. This type of strum is also used in "ska" music.

*On the onbeats, tap the strings with your right hand. This is represented by × in the song below.*

*On the offbeats, strum up.*

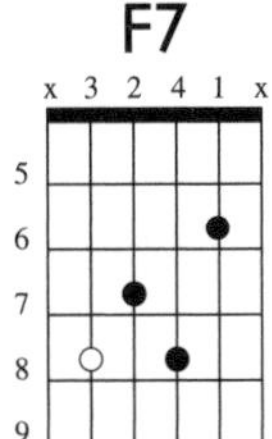


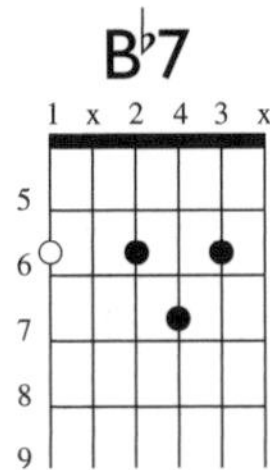


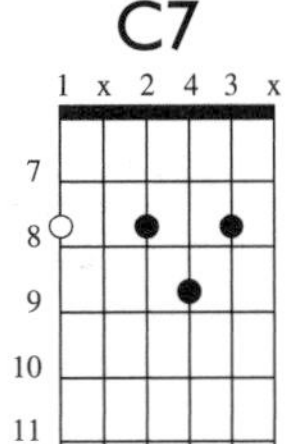

### UPBEAT BLUES IN F

Track 55

× = Unpitched, percussive sound.

*Swing 8ths*

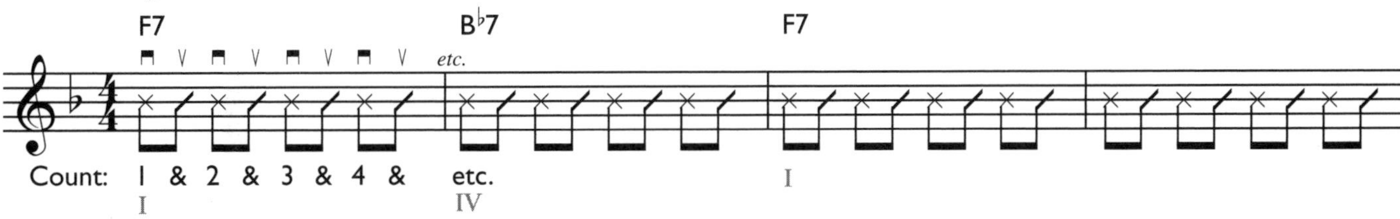


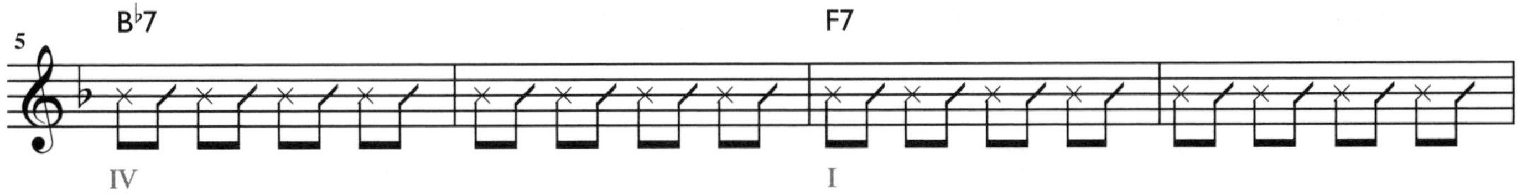


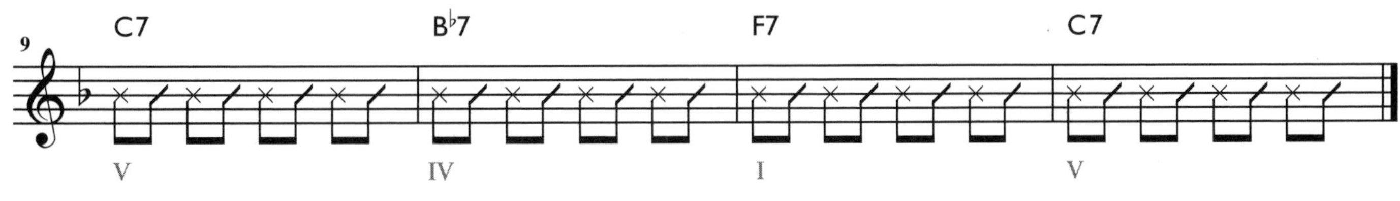

# CHAPTER 13

# Turnarounds

Although many players call the last *four* bars of a blues form the *turnaround,* this term more often refers to a melodic phrase played in the last *two* bars. There are many classic turnarounds that are played over and over again at gigs or jams. They are really fun to play and serve as a signal to other musicians (and to the audience) that a chorus is over and another will be played. As a blues player, it's essential to know the classic turnarounds as they are an integral part of the blues vocabulary.

The examples that follow are all standard turnarounds. They are written in the popular keys of E and A, but eventually, you should learn them in other common keys. Practice them a bit. There will be more information on how to use them at the end of this chapter.

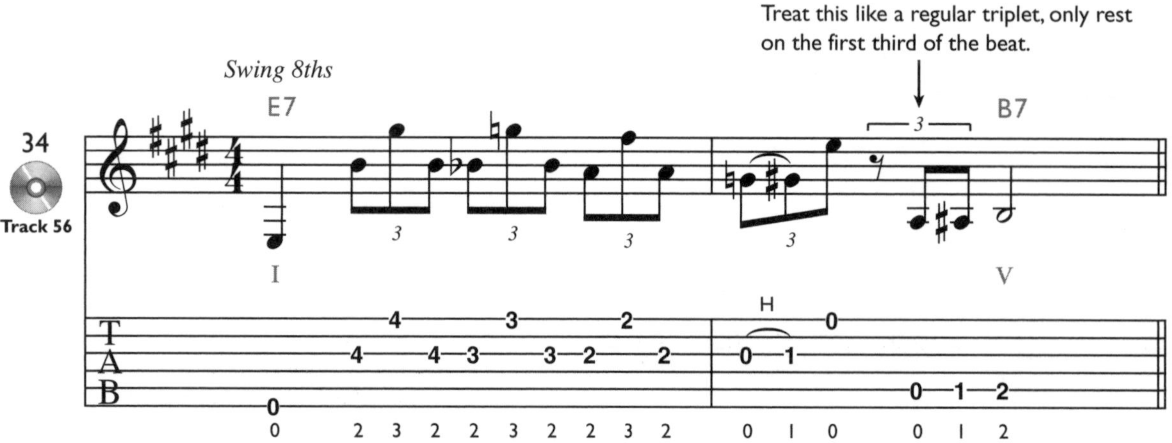

36
Track 58
Swing 8ths
E7
B7
I
V

37
Track 59
Swing 8ths
A7
E7
I
V

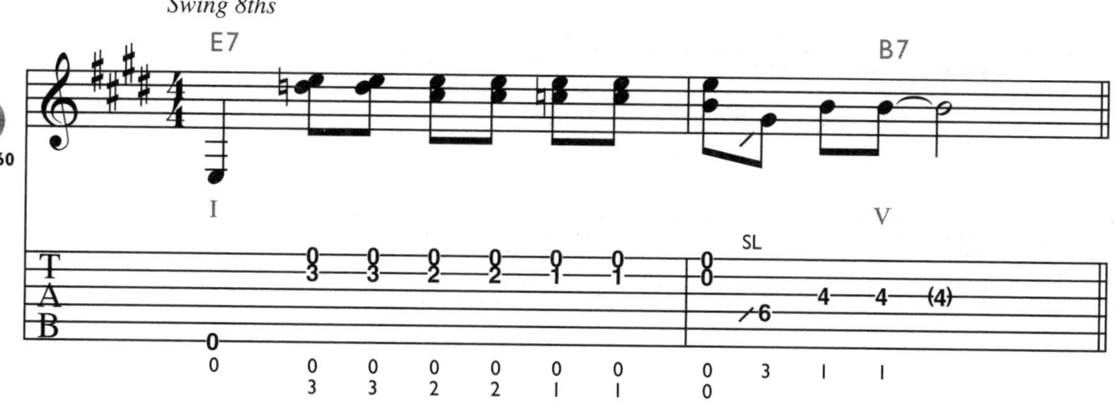
38
Track 60
Swing 8ths
E7
B7
I
V
SL

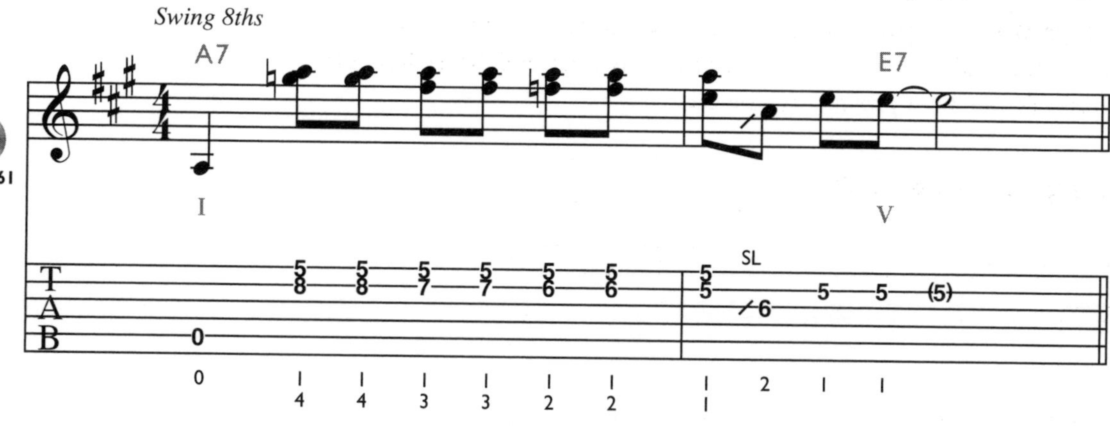
39
Track 61
Swing 8ths
A7
E7
I
V
SL

40

Track 62

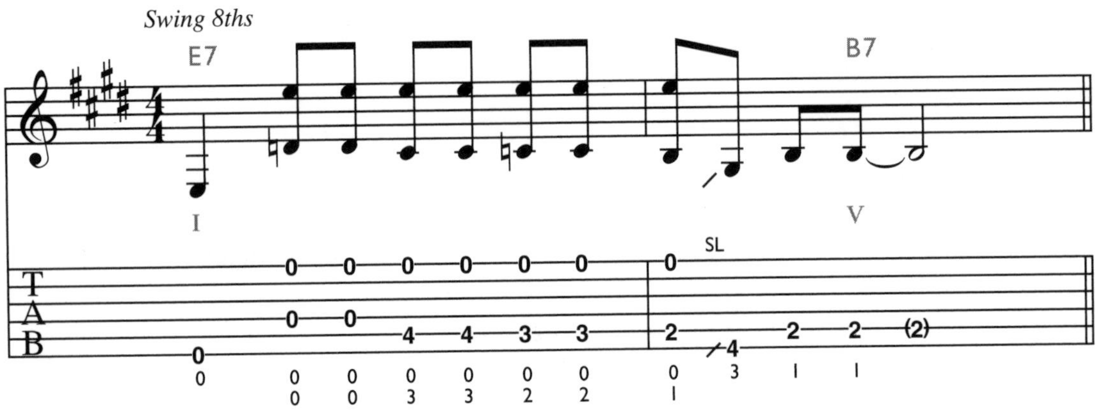
Swing 8ths
E7
B7
I
V
SL
TAB

41

Track 63

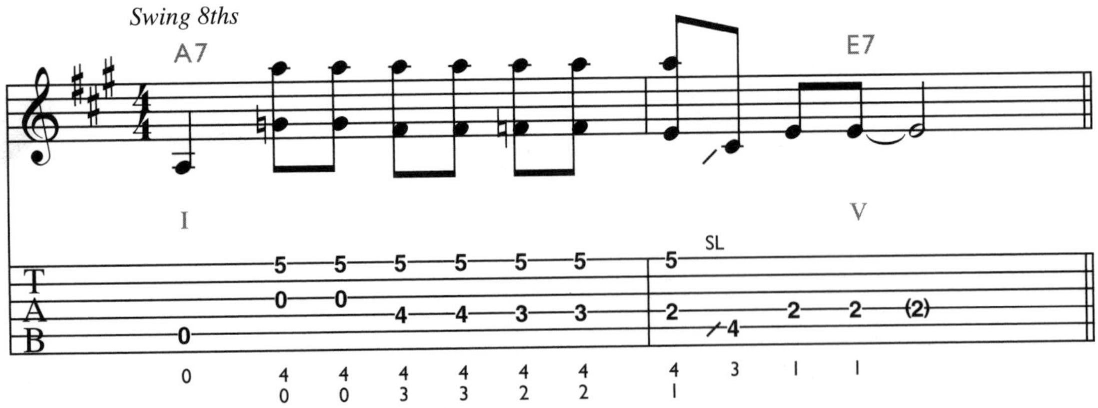
Swing 8ths
A7
E7
I
V
SL
TAB

42

Track 64

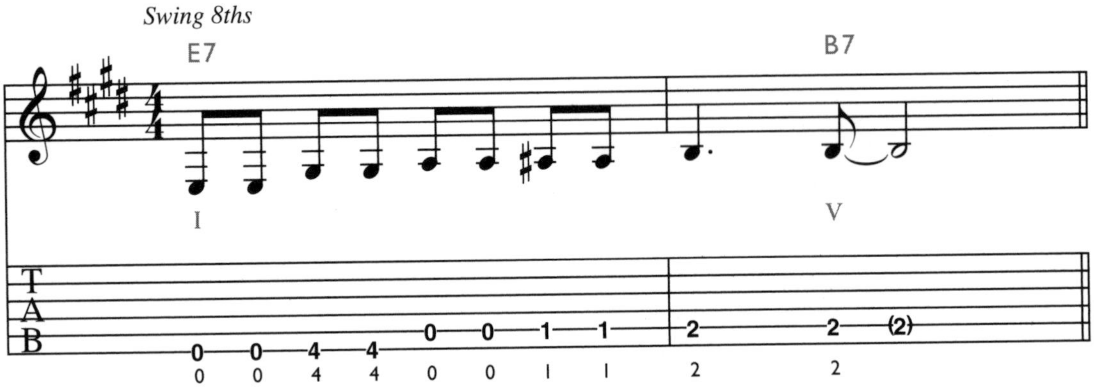
Swing 8ths
E7
B7
I
V
TAB

The above turnaround (example 42) is fairly simple. See if you can transpose it yourself and play it in the key of A. You might want to review page 42 (Closed Forms) for an explanation of transposition. Even though there are open strings in this turnaround, it can be transposed to the key of A very easily. Instead of playing the note pattern on the 6th and 5th strings, play it on the 5th and 4th strings. To see how you did, see below.

### Example 42—Transposed to the Key of A

Swing 8ths
A7
E7
I
V
TAB

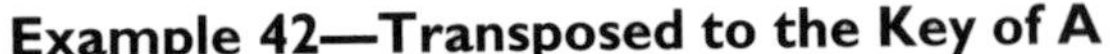

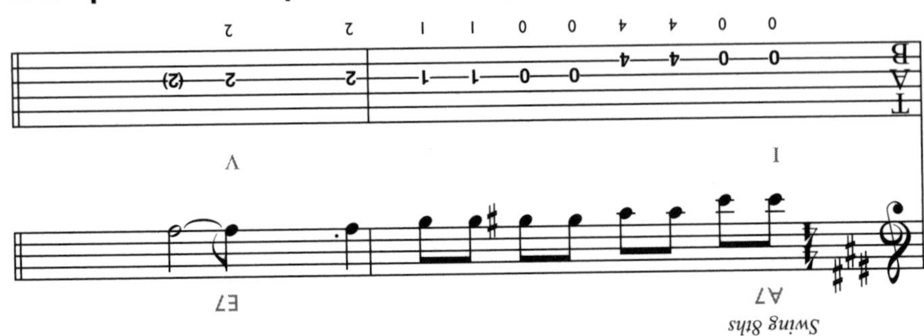

Below is a turnaround consisting entirely of chords; first in E, then in A. Be sure to use the fingerings in the chord diagrams above the staff.

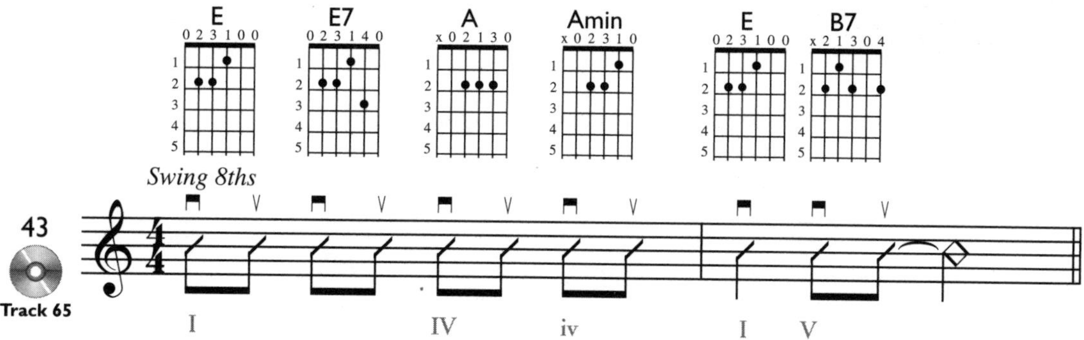


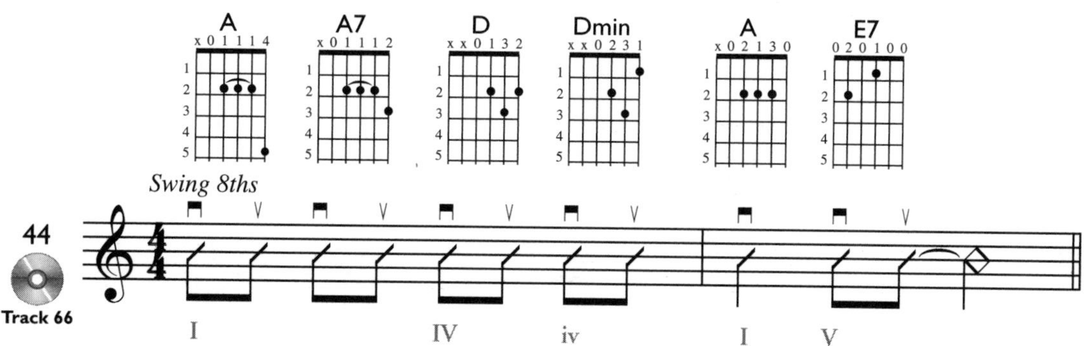


Notice that all the turnarounds are two bars long. Although almost every example begins with a low E or A root-note, the distinctive phrase of each turnaround starts on the second beat.

You can use these classic turnarounds, in the appropriate key, in any piece you play. Play through your chord progression and merely substitute the turnaround for the last two bars. This will work in any of the blues forms you have learned. You can leave the first beat of the turnaround silent; you can strum a I chord in a strumming piece; you can hit a quarter-note 5th if you're playing a shuffle; or just go ahead and play that low root.

Pick your favorite examples and add them to progressions you've learned in this book, and also to any songs you may learn in the future.

You can also use a turnaround as an intro to a piece. It's done often and is an exciting way to kick off a blues tune.

Finally, all the turnarounds in this book can be used as endings if you change the final chord from a V to a I.

# CHAPTER 14

## Riff Style Blues

A *riff* is a short, repeated phrase that is usually played on the lower strings. Many blues pieces are based on riffs. This riff is moved to different starting notes that correspond to the root-notes of the I, IV and V chords of the key.

Our first riff piece is a *minor blues* (a blues progression in which most or all of the chords are minor chords) in the style of the famous tunes, "Help Me," by Sonny Boy Williamson and "Green Onions," by Booker T. & the MG's. We'll take another look at the minor blues in a later chapter (page 82, Minor Blues).

Notice the last three measures. Here you will see *1st* and *2nd endings*. Play through the piece until you come to the 1st repeat sign. Go back and play from the beginning. When you come to the 1st ending, do not play it, but skip over to the 2nd ending and play to the end. Remember to use your balance control to play along with either the chords or the riff on the CD.

### RIFF BLUES IN E MINOR

The riff piece below is in the key of F and based on a boogie woogie pattern. For rhythmic variety, there is a triplet on the fourth beat of each measure. The piece also has a popular ending in which a 9 chord built on the ♭6 (D♭) moves a half step down to a 9 chord built on the 5 (C). This ending even appears in some Elvis songs!

## RIFFIN' IN F

Track 68

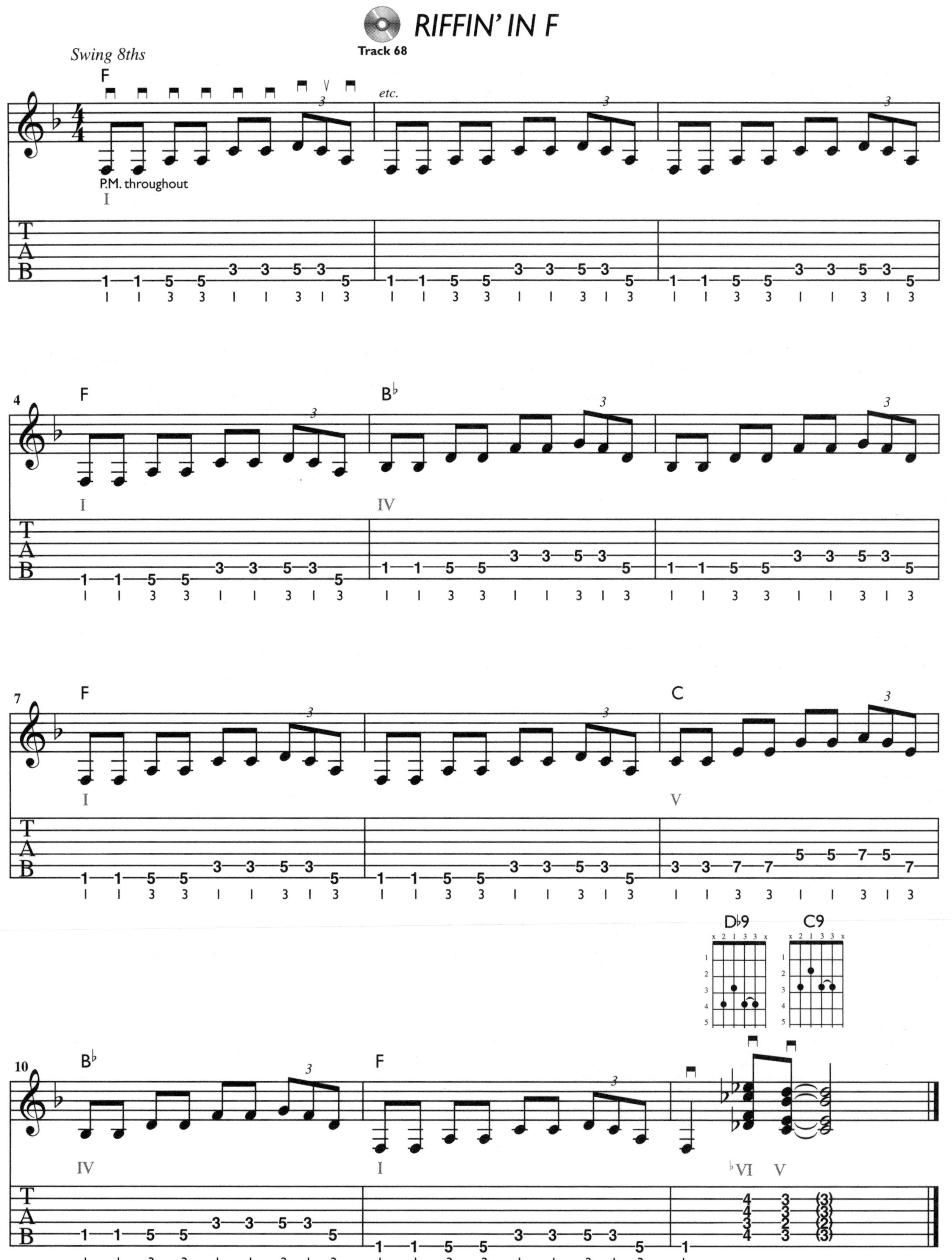

Our next riff blues starts with an octave jump.

# OCTAVE BLUES

Track 69

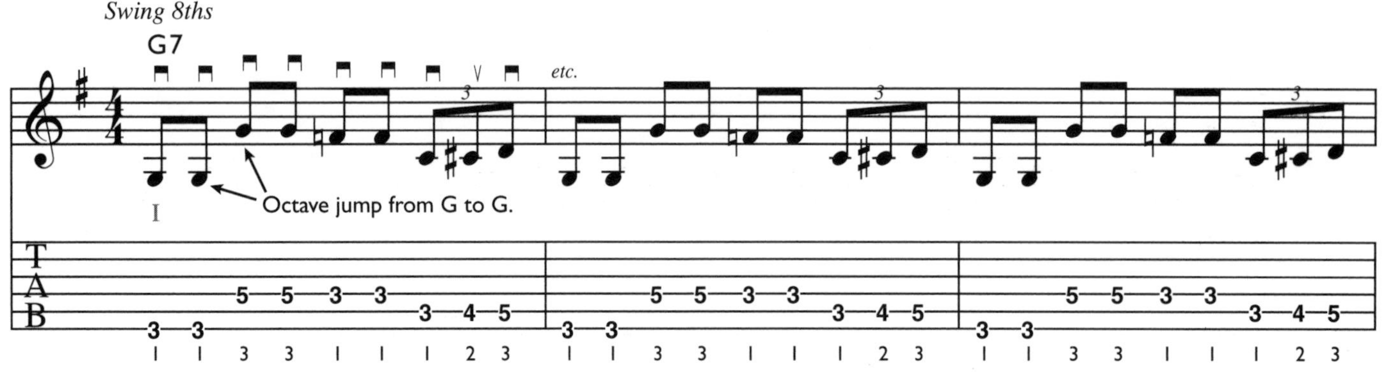


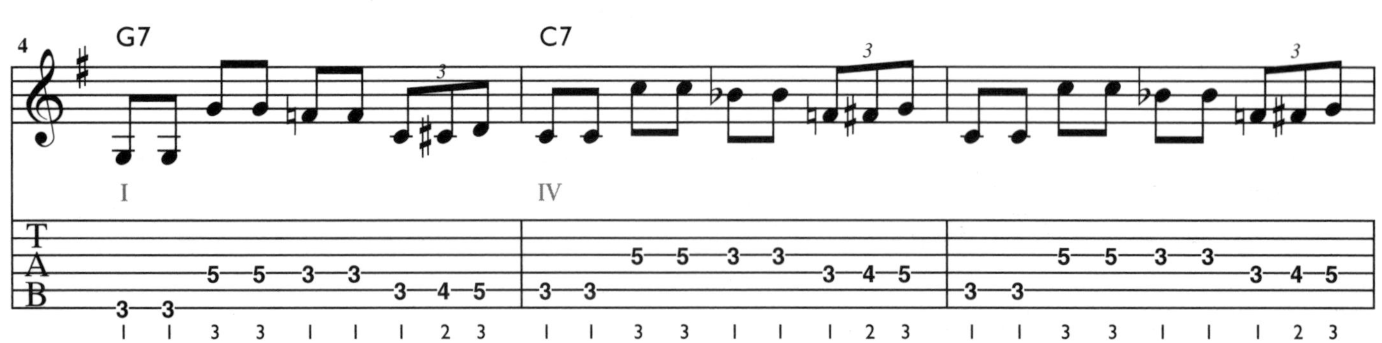


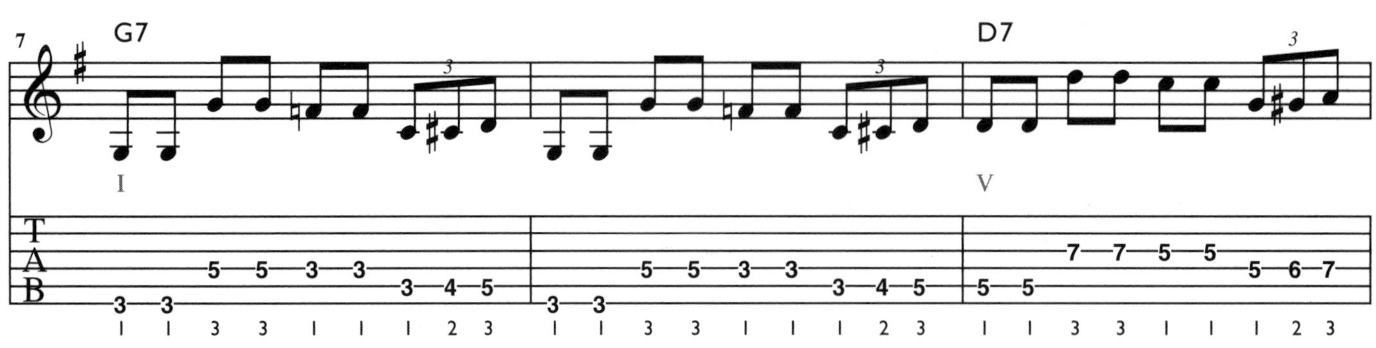

This straight eighth-note piece is a minor blues with a funky sound. Minor 7 chords are incorporated in the riff. The first appearance of the v (notice the lowercase Roman numeral) chord in bar 9 is as a D Minor 7, but in the last bar, the v becomes a V and appears as a D7♯9. The dominant 7♯9 produces another colorful blues sound. It is also used often in funk and rock. Jimi Hendrix used it in "Purple Haze" and other songs. In fact, some people refer to the 7♯9 as "the Hendrix chord."

## FUNKY BLUES IN G MINOR

Track 70

# CHAPTER 15

## Moveable Two-String Patterns

In Chapter 4 (pages 26–27), we discussed shuffles that were based on alternating perfect 5ths and major 6ths. Each of those patterns were based on open-string root-notes. In this section, we will see how we can transpose these sounds to fretted roots. This will allow us to play in the shuffle style in any key.

The following "5" and "6" shapes have their roots on the 6th and 5th strings and are in the key of G. In the key of G, the I chord is G, the IV chord is C and the V chord is D.

**Root-6 Shapes**
(root on the 6th string)

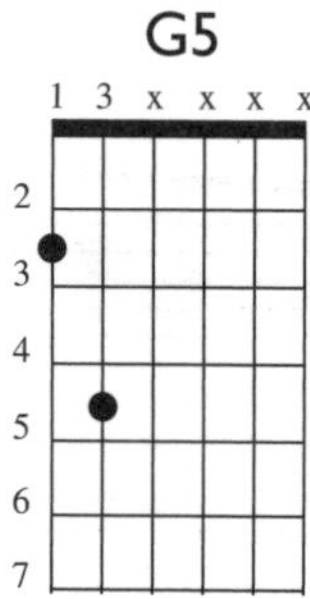


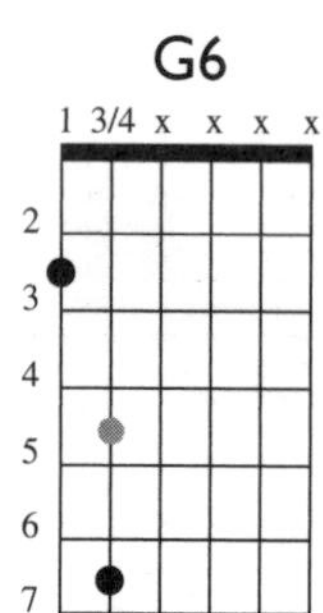


**Root-5 Shapes**
(root on the 5th string)

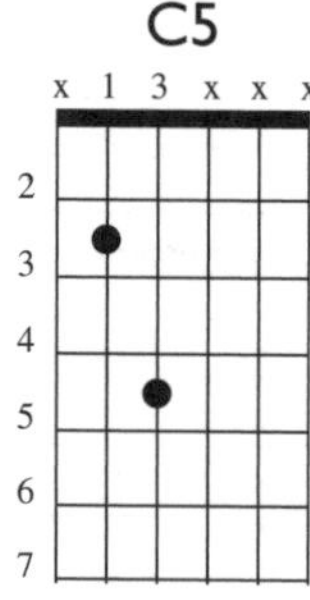


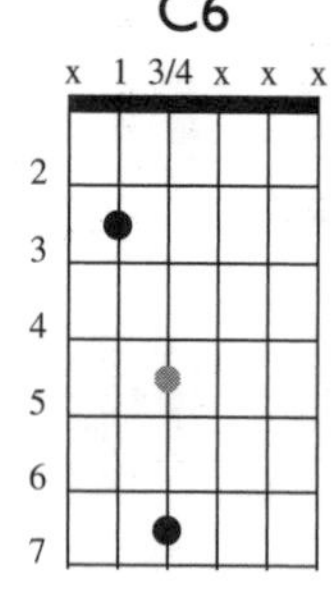


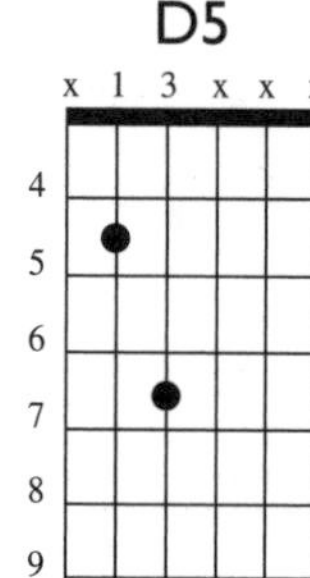


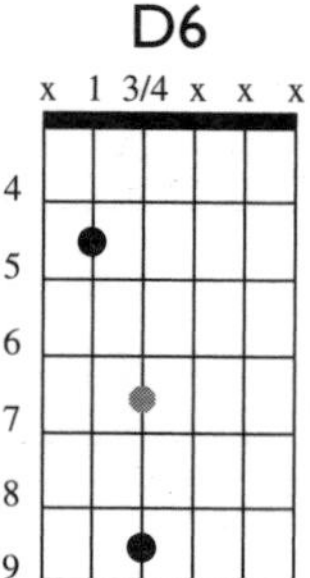


It's easy to change keys using the shapes on this page. If you use the root-6 shape as the I chord—anywhere on the neck—the IV will always be a root-5 shape on the same fret. If you move the IV chord two frets higher, you get the V.

The shuffle below is in the key of G. The turnaround is based on a dominant 7, three-note fingering that descends in half steps. This is followed by a 9 chord built on the ♭6 (E♭9) that moves to a 9 chord built on the 5 (D9).

This piece does not include the move to the ♭7 (see page 30). Some people, especially those with smaller hands, have trouble stretching to this colorful note. Try adding it in if you can. It's always one fret higher than the 6. If you can't reach it yet, practice stretching with your 4th finger and you will get it eventually.

## SHUFFLE IN G

Track 71

Now we will use our moveable two-string shapes to play a piece with straight eighth notes. It's in the key of B♭ and in the style of Chuck Berry's "Johnny B. Goode." Some of Jimmy Reed's famous songs are also in this rockin' blues, straight eighth-note style.

## CHUCK'S BLUES

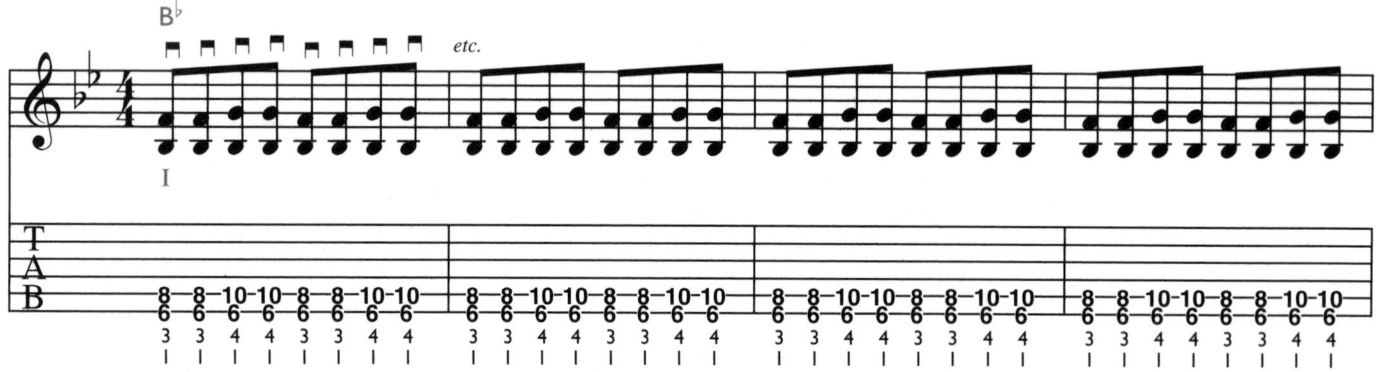


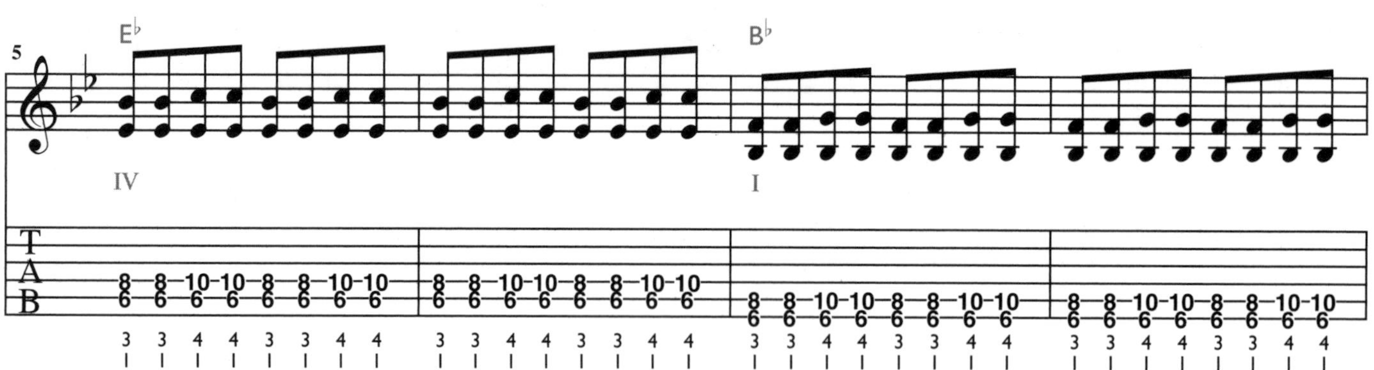


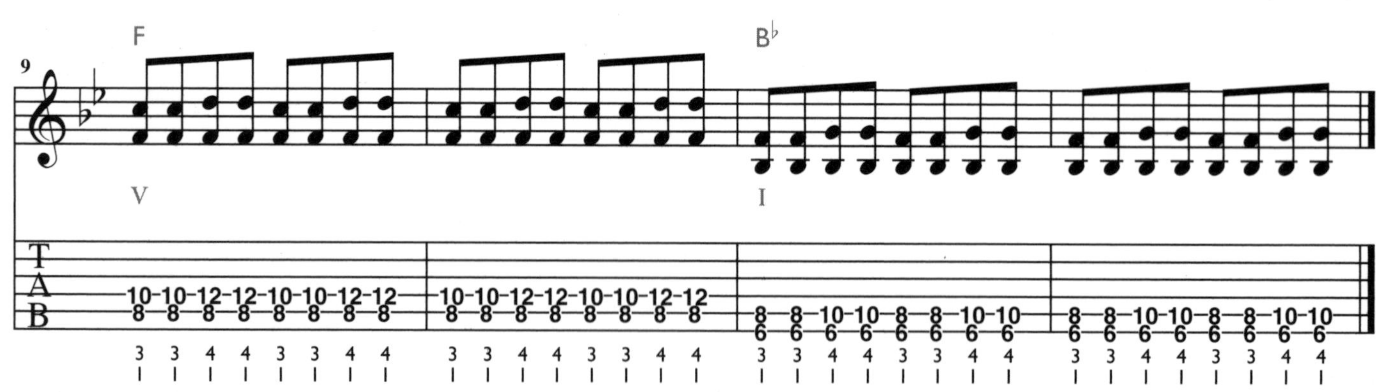

Sometimes the notes of these two-string patterns are played separately. This technique is used in the Most Common Blues in E below. Notice there is a note before the first full measure of music. This is a *pickup*. Count one full measure of four beats, then come in with the pickup on the "&" of beat 4. Theoretically, the missing beats of the pickup measure come from the beats of the last measure, which is incomplete.

## SHUFFLIN' IN E

Track 73

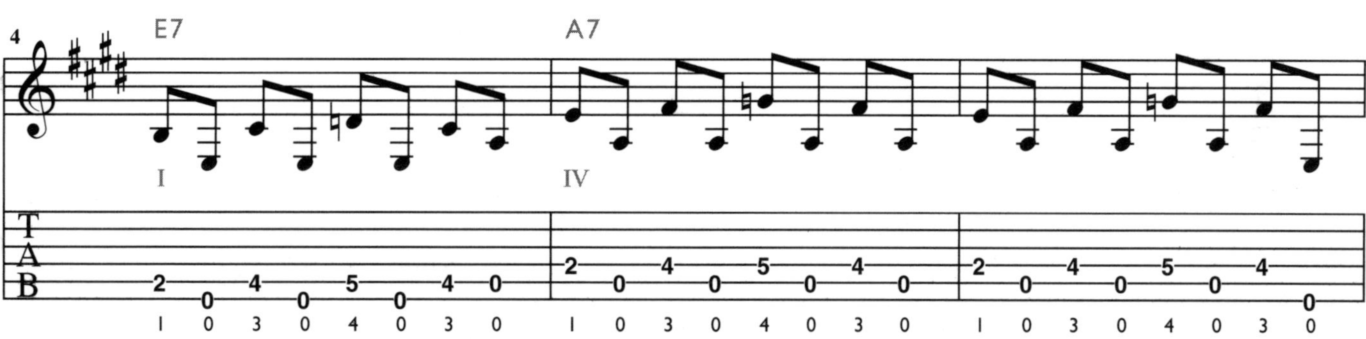


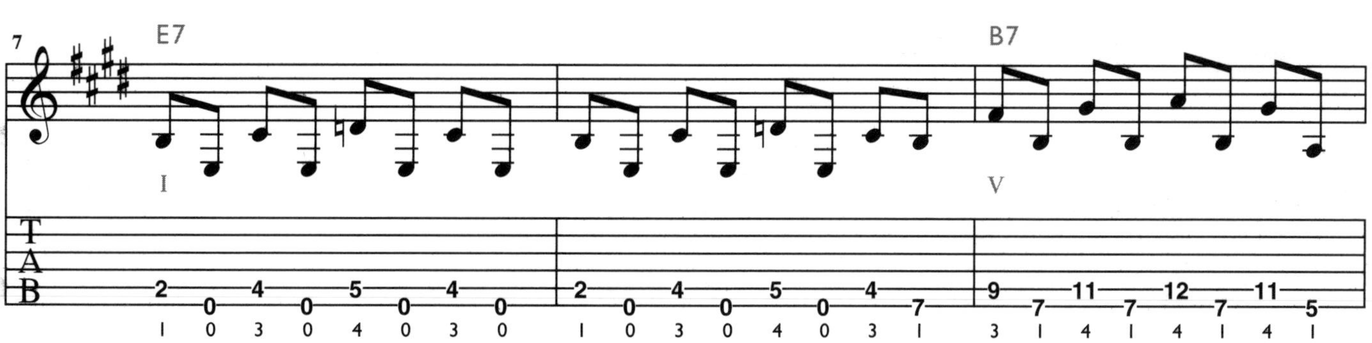


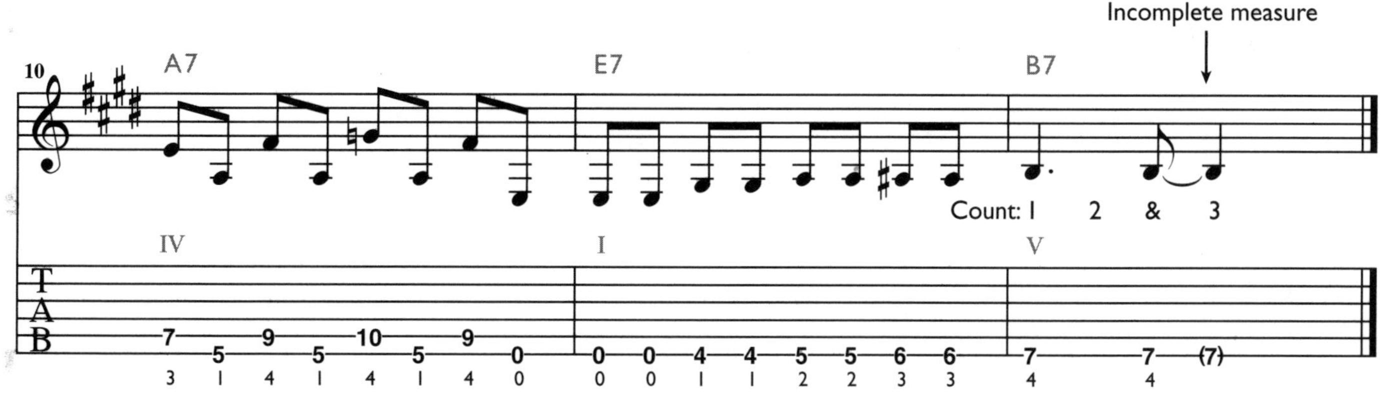

# CHAPTER 16

## Barre Chords

Barre chords, first introduced on page 46, are an essential tool for a guitarist. Remember, these are chords in which one finger, usually the 1st, lies flat over a fret and presses multiple strings. They are used in blues and almost every other guitar style. They are moveable shapes—closed voicings—that can be played on any fret. They can be a little tricky to play correctly but they will have to be mastered.

Start working on these only when you are comfortable with the other chords in this book. At that point, your left-hand fingers will have the strength and agility needed to play barre chords.

Below are all the important barre chord shapes. Practice each shape on various frets up and down the neck. Listen to each note in the chord and adjust your fingers to get a clear sound from each.

A barre is indicated with a curved line ——— over the strings to be barred. Remember, hollow dots indicate the roots of the chords.

**Root-6 Barre Chords**

Major

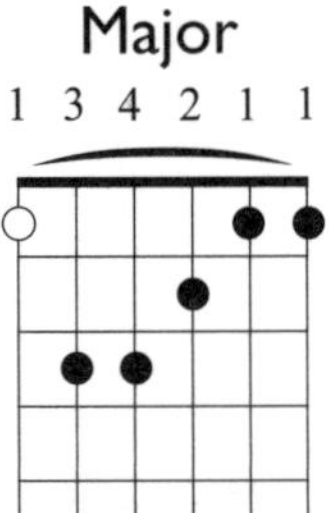


Minor

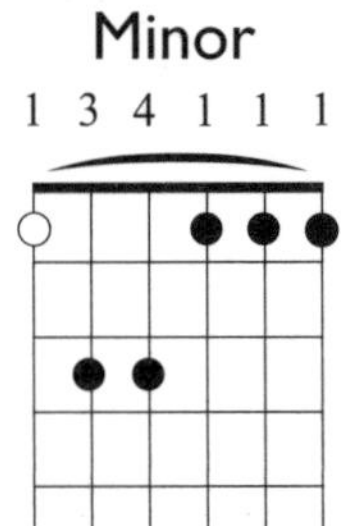


7

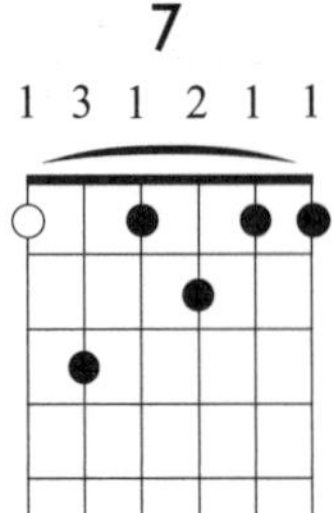


Minor 7

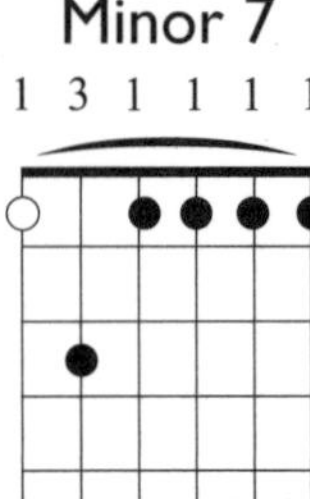


**Root-5 Barre Chords**

Major

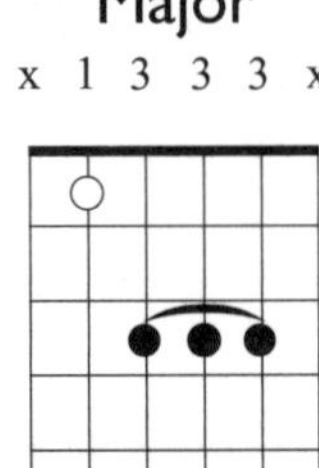


Minor

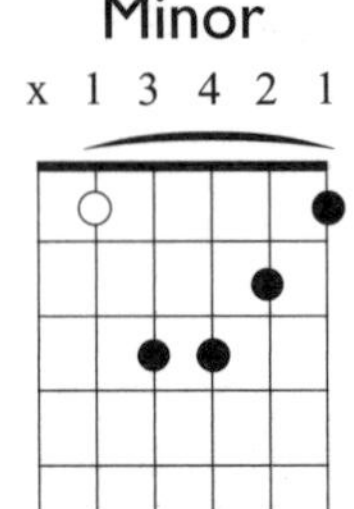


7

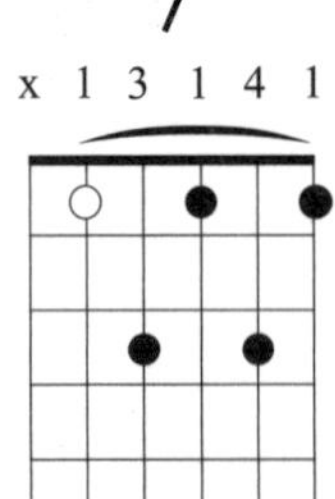


Minor 7

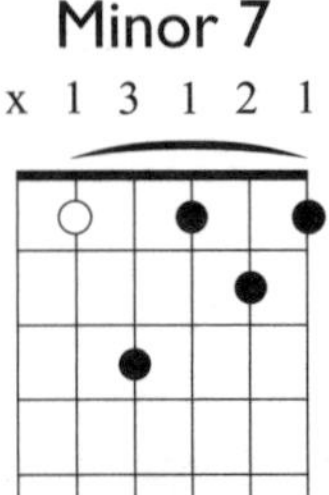

This piece is in the key of A♭, but you should try it in other keys as well. Take note, there are two different fingerings for A♭7. They are numbered ① and ② so you know which to use.

You will be using dominant 7 barre chords, but it is a good idea to practice blues progressions using major, minor and minor 7 barre chords as well. Start with a root-6 I chord, and the IV will always be a root-5 shape on the same fret. The V will always be two frets higher than the IV.

Here are the chords you will need for this progression.

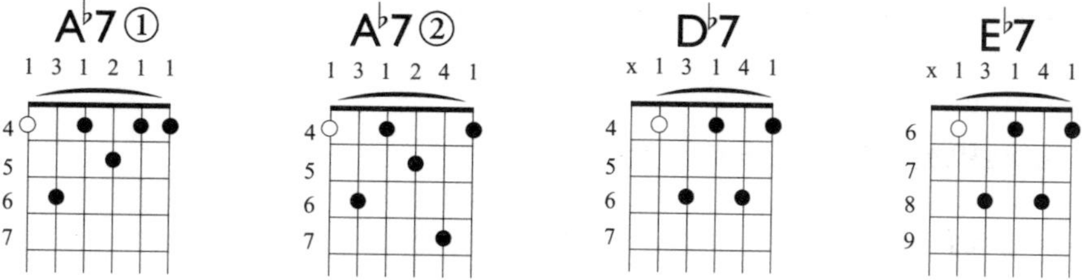

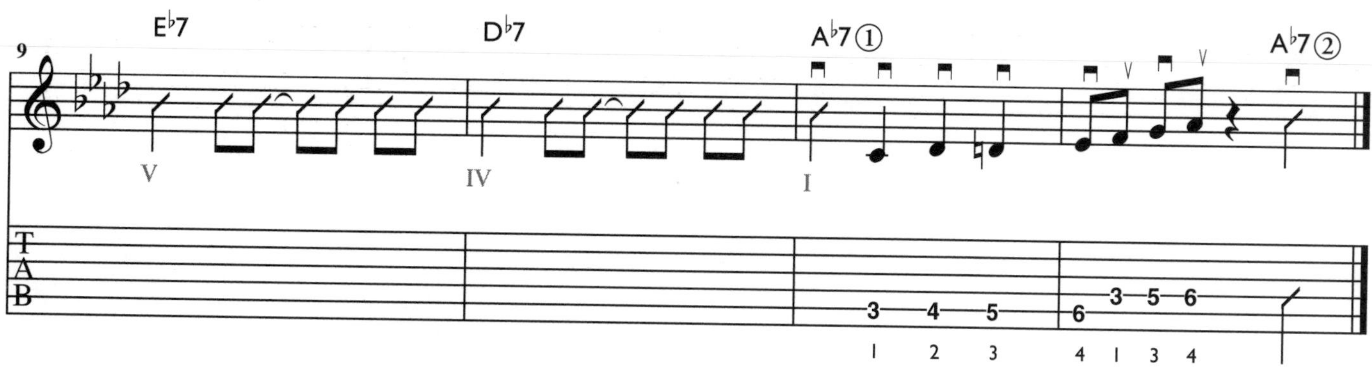

# CHAPTER 17

# Eight-Bar Blues

Although the 12-bar pattern is by far the most popular blues form, the *eight-bar blues* is also fairly common. This is a blues form made up of eight measures.

This following tune is in the style of "Key to the Highway," a blues classic by Bill Broonzy that has been recorded by many artists.

The triplet on the fourth beat of each measure adds rhythmic variety to our piece.

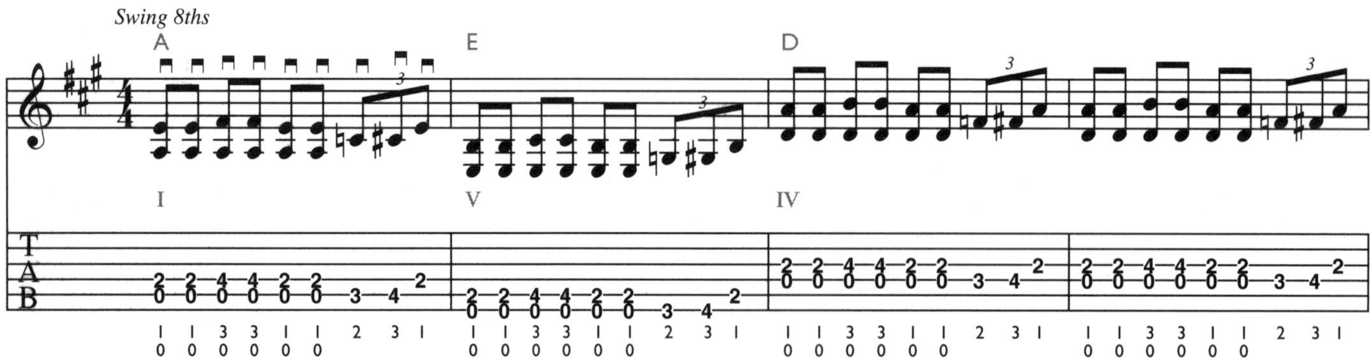


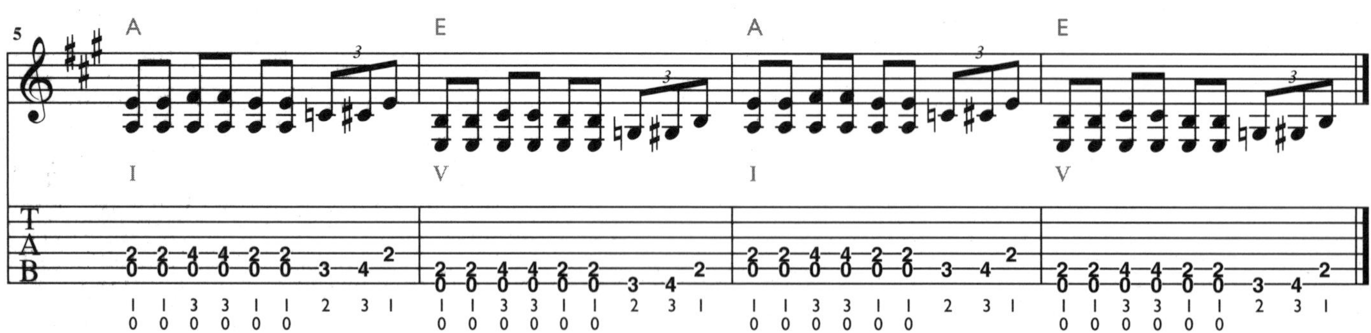

"How Long Blues" was a huge hit for the influential duo of Leroy Carr and Scrapper Blackwell in 1928. It is a standard, or a "must know" tune for any blues player. This next song is in the style of "How Long Blues," but is based on a version of the song by Leadbelly.

Leadbelly was a Texas musician who led a colorful life. He had a very strong guitar sound. Known as the "King of the 12-String Guitar," he strummed down on the lower strings with his thumb, and up on the upper strings with his fingers, or index finger. Try this approach with the next piece. When it's comfortable for you, try it with other songs too. It's a great technique for creating a slightly rough, down-home sound.

Notice there are two different fingerings for the E7 chord.

## TOO LONG BLUES

Track 76

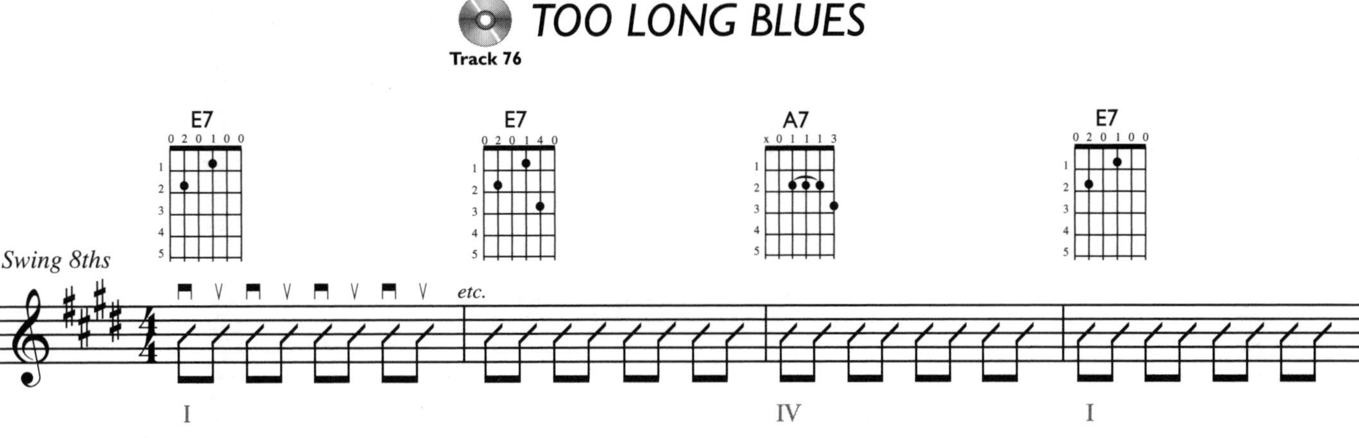


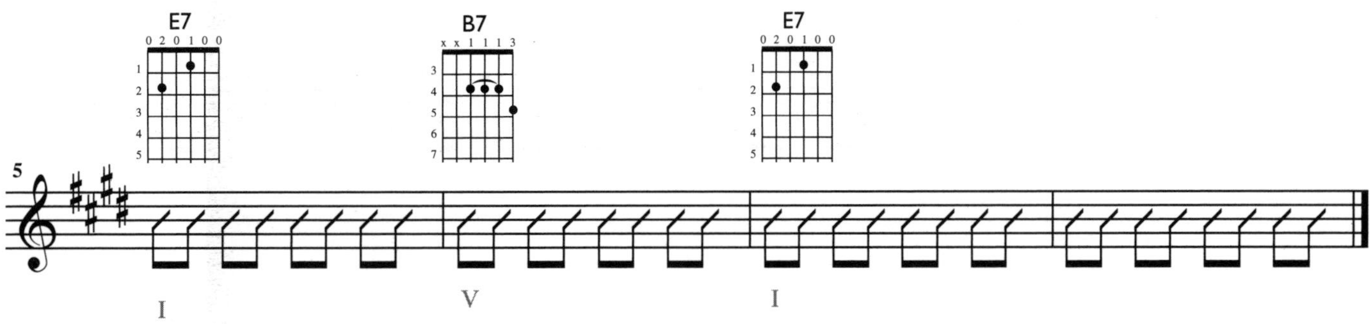

# CHAPTER 18

## Minor Blues

Remember, a *minor blues* is a progression in which most or all of the chords are minor chords. As you may have noticed in the minor blues pieces we have already played (pages 70, 73), they have a very distinct sound and are a great alternative to the major and dominant 7 sound we get from most other blues. Some would say they give us a deeper, moodier and more soulful sound.

The following progression is composed entirely of minor chords. The i chord is Amin; the iv chord is Dmin; the v chord is Emin.

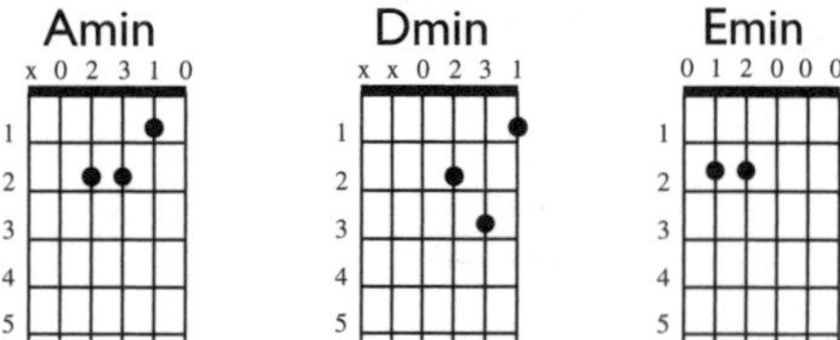


### MINOR BLUES IN A

Track 77

Although it will be more difficult, you can try the above minor blues with the barre chords below.

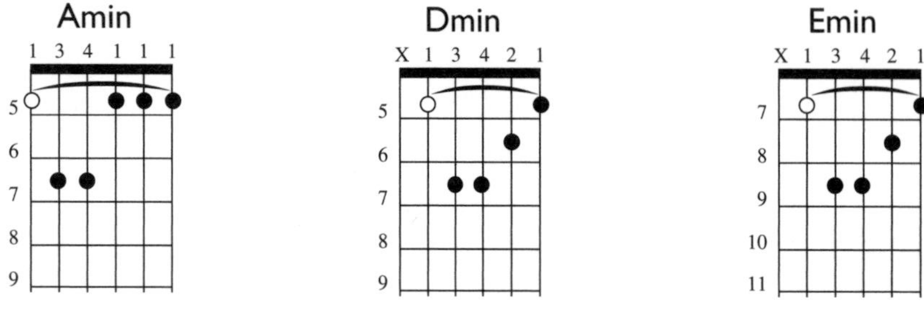

Though in our last piece we used Emin, it is standard practice in minor blues to make the v a dominant 7 chord. This would make the Emin an E7. Our next piece uses this approach.

Minor 7 chords are used instead of the straight minor chords. When you play the chord voicings in this piece, be sure to mute any open strings. Remember, this is done by lightly touching them with the fingers that are fretting notes on adjacent strings. The strum for this piece is similar to the strum you learned on page 62, with the exception that there is a quarter-note strum on the last beat of each measure.

Amin7 Dmin7 E7

## THREE-STRUM BLUES

Track 78

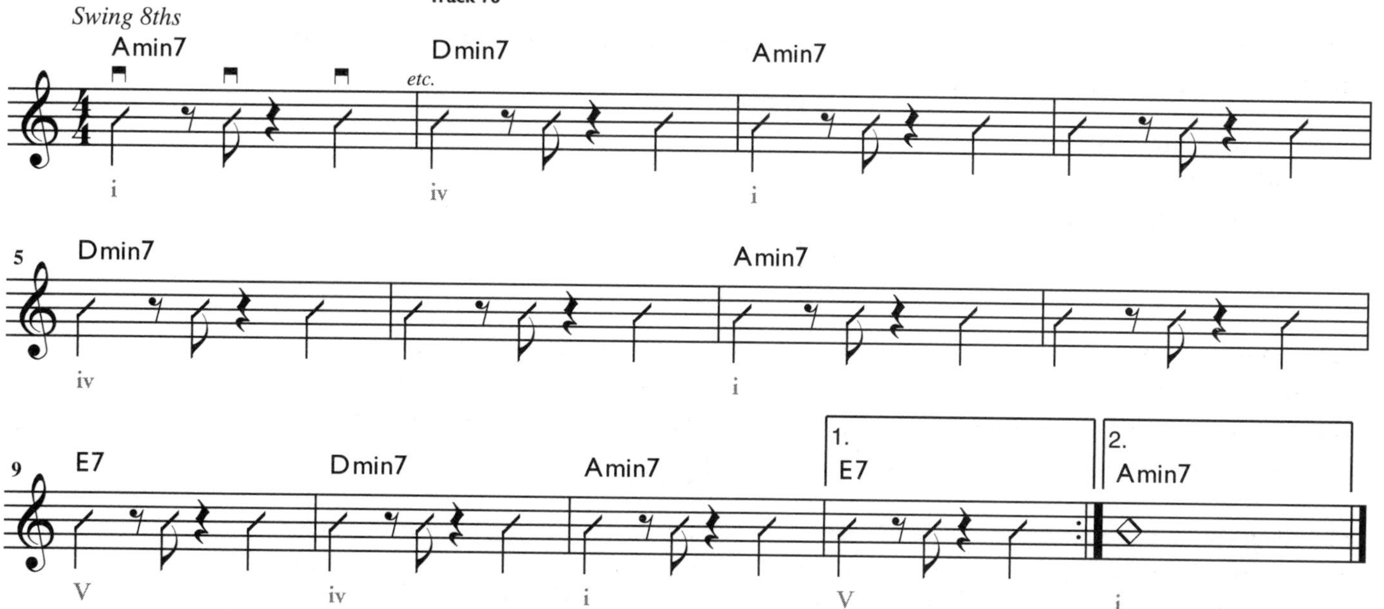


This next progression is in the style of B. B. King's "The Thrill Is Gone." It has minor 7 chords and even a G Major 7 chord (which is a ♭VI). The Bmin7 and F♯7 will sound best with the barre chord voicings to the right. However, if these chords are too difficult for you at this point, you can use the alternative chords next to them.

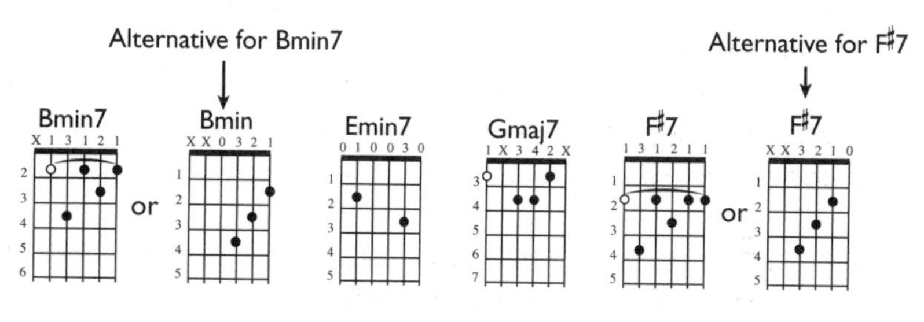

## BLUES FOR B. B.

Track 79

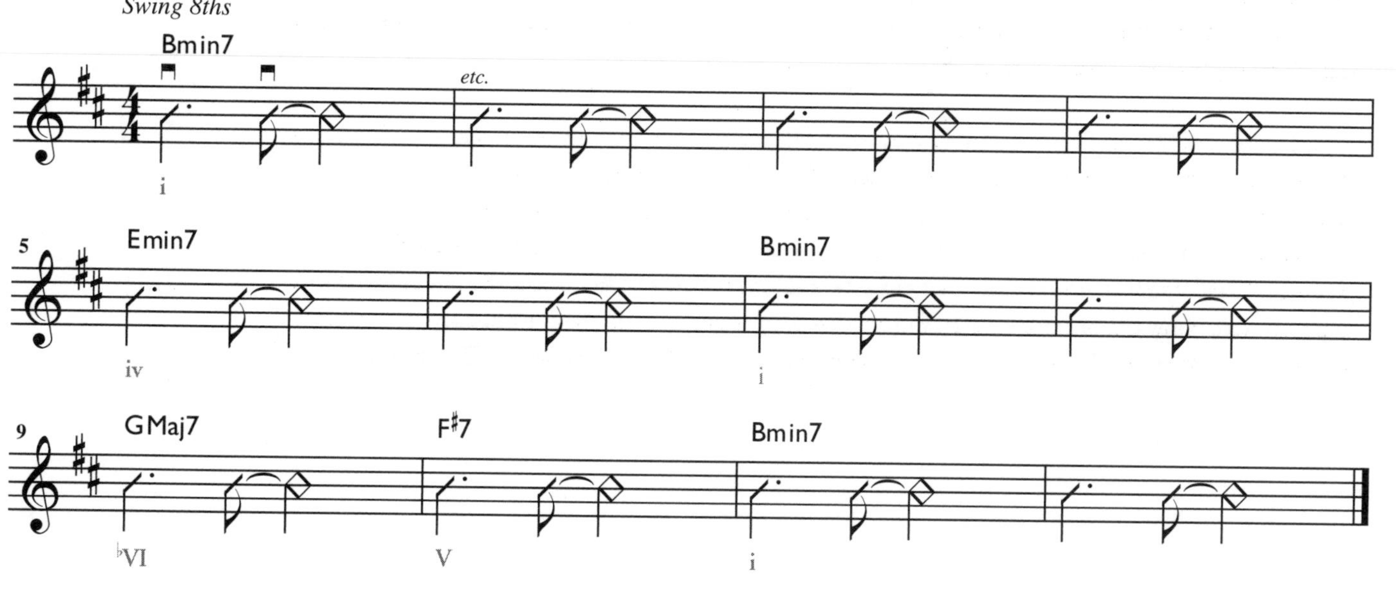

# CHAPTER 19

# Fingerstyle Blues

In this chapter, the basics of fingerstyle blues technique will be introduced. All the early pioneers of the blues were fingerstyle players. Playing fingerstyle is a fun and rewarding way to play.

Let's start by talking about the right hand. It's traditional to use Spanish terms for the right-hand fingers, and these are then abbreviated:

- *pulgar (p)* for thumb
- *indice (i)* for index
- *medio (m)* for middle
- *anular (a)* for ring

Your index *(i)*, middle *(m)* and ring *(a)* fingers are assigned to the upper three strings. Your thumb should cover the notes on the lower three strings. In standard music notation, notes played with the thumb are written with the stems going down. This is the rule for all the pieces in this chapter, and is the general approach for most fingerstyle playing.

Most fingerstyle blues pieces are based on chords. A chord is held with the left hand and the right hand picks notes from it in various rhythms. The notes from these chords need to be held; they should continue to ring out even after they are plucked. This is important because you will see individual notes in the music. Do not try to play the pieces by jumping from one individual note to another. Instead, hold the correct chord for that measure, and all the notes you need will be there. In more melodic pieces, like "Blues for Mississippi John" (page 87), the upper notes cannot be held, but be sure to let the bass notes sustain. In general, holding notes as long as possible (especially the notes played by the thumb) will give you a full sound.

When practicing, it's a good idea to repeat each bar a few times. This will get the phrases under your fingers and help you master the piece.

**Minor Blues for Rev. Gary—Preparation**

Our first fingerstyle piece has a right-hand pattern that is repeated in every measure. The thumb *(p)* alternates between two of the lower strings in each chord; this is called an *alternating bass.* When using alternating bass in the blues, the bass notes played with the thumb on beats 2 and 4 are often slightly accented: 1, **2,** 3, **4.**

Watch the right-hand fingering (indicated next to the notes in standard music notation) and the left-hand fingering (indicated under the TAB staff)—and keep it steady. The progression is a 16-bar minor blues that is based on the classic song, "Motherless Children." Like all blues standards, it was played by many performers. Rev. Gary Davis's rendition is probably the most popular. Our arrangement is not even close to the complexity of his, but it has the same chord progression. Many other songs are based on this progression. If we change each minor chord to a major or dominant 7, we get the chord progression for "When the Saints Go Marching In."

# MINOR BLUES FOR REV. GARY

Track 80

### Blues for Mississippi John—Preparation

Learn to play pieces by Mississippi John Hurt. You'll love them. He played in the alternating bass style and sang up-tempo and fun songs. Also, his music is easier to play than the work of many other famous blues performers, so it's a good choice for a beginner.

This 12-bar blues on page 87 is typical of his pieces in G. Accent the second and fourth beats and watch the slide up to the 7th fret in bar 9.

In bars 5 and 6, you'll need to hold the notes of a C chord while stretching your 4th finger to fret the E♭. If this stretch is too difficult in the 1st *position* (position indicates where your 1st finger is located—in this case, the 1st fret), you can place a *capo* on the neck and play the piece in a higher position. A capo is a type of clamp that a guitarist can place on the neck to change the pitch of the music they are playing. Capos allow you to change keys without learning new fingerings. The frets get smaller as we move up the neck, so stretches are easier in higher positions. Practice your stretches by moving the capo lower as time goes on. As you play more and more, your fingers will become more agile, flexible and capable of longer stretches.

PHOTO • COURTESY OF VANGUARD

***Mississippi John Hurt** began playing guitar in 1903. A farm laborer, he developed his unique fingerpicking style in obscurity. It wasn't until the folk revival of the 1950s and 1960s that he received recognition by a mass audience. Suddenly, he found himself making more money than he ever thought possible. Until months before his death, he continued to record and perform as an artist who was in his prime.*

## BLUES FOR MISSISSIPPI JOHN

Track 81

### Keep on Pickin'—Preparation

The early acoustic players like Robert Johnson, Blind Lemon Jefferson, Blind Blake and others played 12-bar progressions. They also played many songs based on other common patterns. The 16-bar chord sequence in "Keep On Pickin'" (page 89) is found in many songs including "Keep on Truckin'." This tune was played by many early players and was also recorded by Hot Tuna. Arlo Guthrie's "Alice's Restaurant" is also based on a similar progression. This style, which can be called *ragtime blues,* has a bouncy alternating bass—and it has more chords and quicker chord changes than 12-bar pieces.

For the C chords, the alternating bass starts with a C on the 5th string, moves to E on the 4th string, to G on the 6th string and back to E on the 4th string. To fret the G, just lift your 3rd finger off the C and place it on the 6th string, 3rd fret. We could finger the C chord with our 4th finger on the C and 3rd finger on the G and hold all the notes at the same time. If we move the 3rd finger from string to string, however, we will get a bass sound that is more characteristic of this type of piece.

Below are the chords you will need to play "Keep On Pickin'." The fingering for the F chord—with the left-hand thumb playing the root—is common, but if your thumb can't make the reach, use the barre fingering for the F instead.

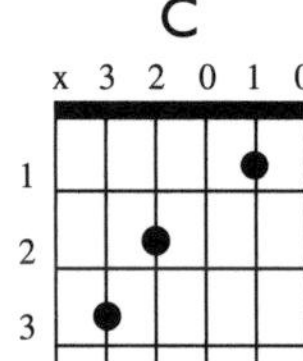


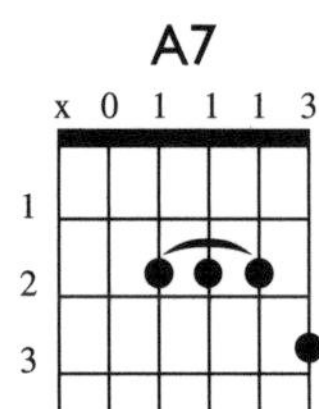


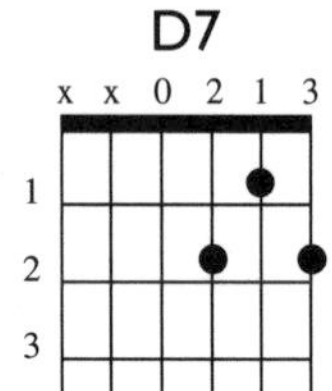


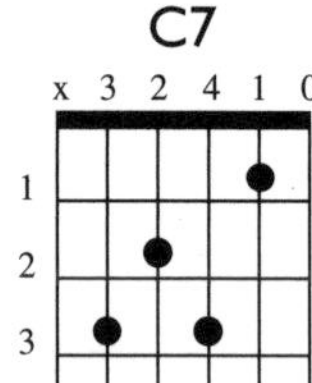


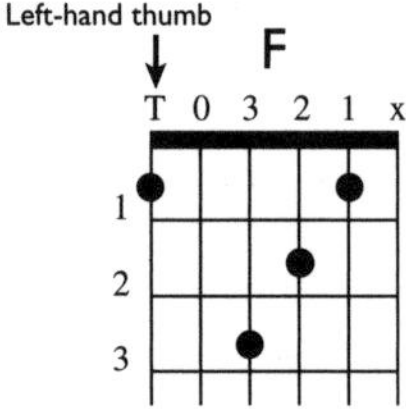


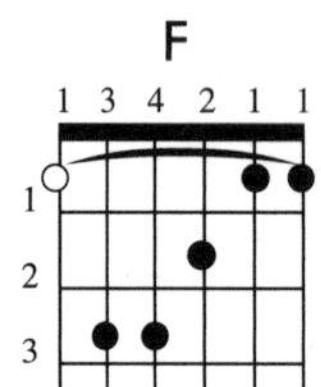


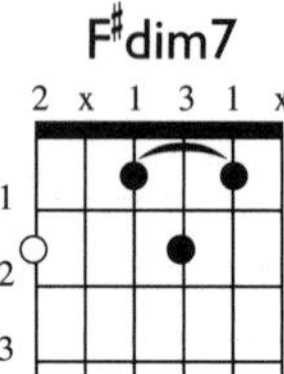

# KEEP ON PICKIN'

Track 82

*Swing 8ths*

**Blues for Lightnin'—Preparation**

Most fingerstyle blues pieces can be divided into two categories. In one category, pieces are based on the alternating bass. In the other, the thumb repeats a root-note on the lower strings. This style is sometimes called *Texas blues* and was used by the great Lightnin' Hopkins. Unlike ragtime blues, this style is not totally based on chords. Instead, a player will keep a steady beat on a low note and play melodic phrases or licks on the upper strings. There will be a few chords added here and there. This way of playing creates a full sound and is excellent for playing solo. When you get this going, you'll really sound like a blues player.

Texas blues is almost always played in the keys of E and A because in these keys, most of our important root notes are on open strings. This allows our left hand to play phrases on the upper strings in any position.

"Blues for Lightnin'" is based on the E Minor Pentatonic scale and contains a few popular blues licks. Notice that in measure 3, the E-note is played on the open 1st string and also on the 2nd string, 5th fret. Alternating between an open note and the unison fretted on the next string is a popular blues technique. Be careful with the slides, pull-offs and vibrato in this piece. It is a good idea to practice them separately.

Play the upper-string three-note E7, A7 and B7 chords by brushing upward lightly with your index finger. Be sure to keep your thumb steady on the repeated root-notes. No one will call the "blues police" if you miss a note, but it will not sound as good.

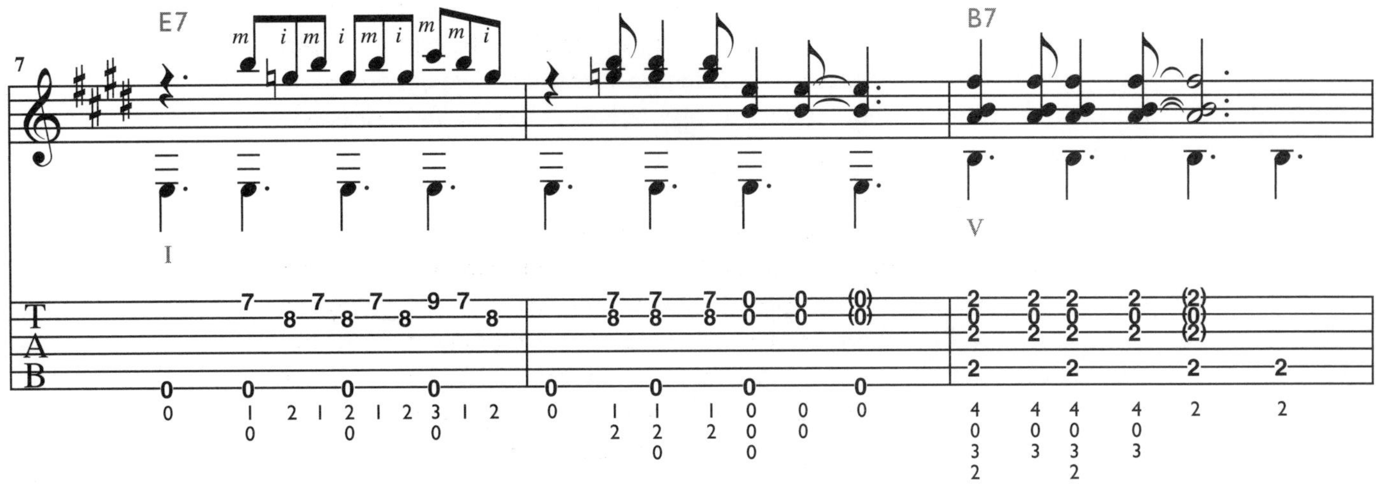


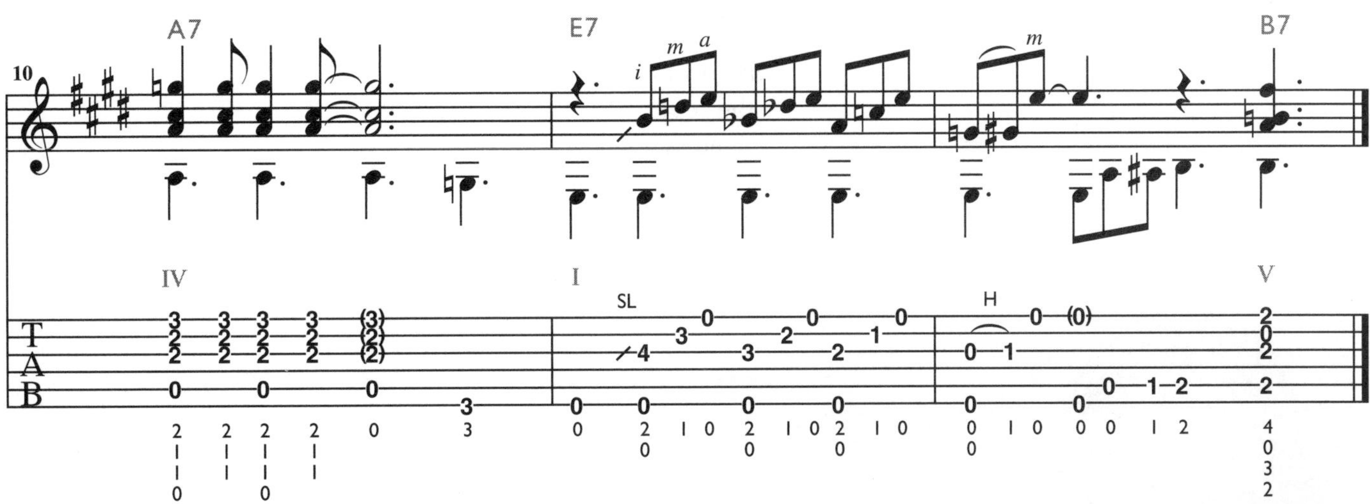

COURTESY OF INSTITUTE OF JAZZ STUDIES, RUTGERS UNIVERSITY

***Jimmie Rodgers,*** *who left the railroad and began his musical career in the 1920s, is nowadays called "The Father of Country Music." However, even a title that prestigious only begins to address the scope of his accomplishments. His influence has been felt not only in country music, but also in the folk and blues music that were a major part of his unique style.*

**Boogie Woogie Time—Preparation**

We covered boogie woogie style in Chapter 8 (page 42). Now we will play a boogie woogie pattern in which the thumb plays the lower strings while chords are played on the upper strings. It should almost sound like two people playing at the same time. Since the parts are so independent, you will probably find this piece more interesting than the others in this section. Boogie woogie pieces are usually played at fast tempos. As usual, have patience and keep at it. When you master this piece, you'll love to play it, and it will be an impressive addition to your repertoire.

Practice each section of the piece separately and keep the tempo very slow at first. Playing the phrases slowly will get them under your fingers. It will help you memorize them and allow them to "sink in." Throughout measures 1–6, you'll need to hold down the G♯ on the 3rd string while other fingers stretch to the 4th fret for certain bass notes. If at the moment this is too much of a stretch, use the capo and play the piece starting on a higher fret. Another option is to omit the G♯ and just play the open 1st and 2nd strings. This will not sound as good, but will be much easier. You can always add the G♯ later, when your stretching improves.

Unlike "Blues for Lightnin'," here we want to use our *i*, *m* and *a* fingers to pluck the upper strings for a cleaner sound.

*To many, the music of **Robert Johnson** is the epitome of the blues. In 1930, partly inspired by bluesman Son House, Johnson left the world of sharecropping to become a full-time musician. In his short career, he recorded 29 songs. These intense recordings represent some of the most influential blues music ever produced.*

# BOOGIE WOOGIE TIME

Track 84

# APPENDIX

## Chord Fingerings

The chords on this page—along with the barre chord fingerings in Chapter 16 (page 78)—will get you through most blues situations.

### Dominant 7 Fingerings—Open or 1st position

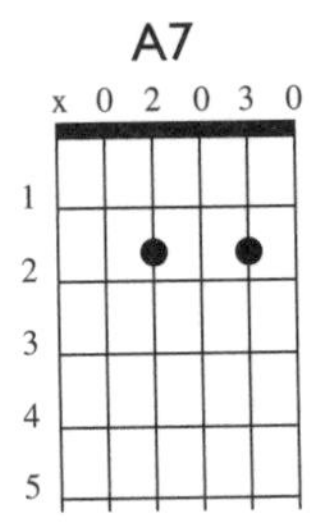

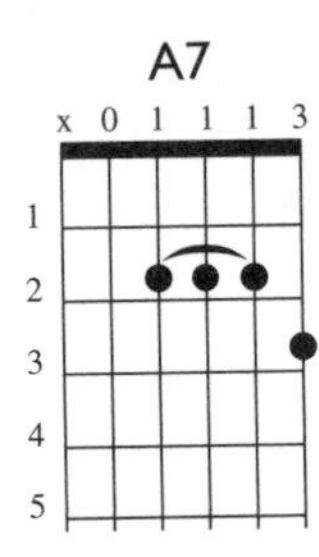

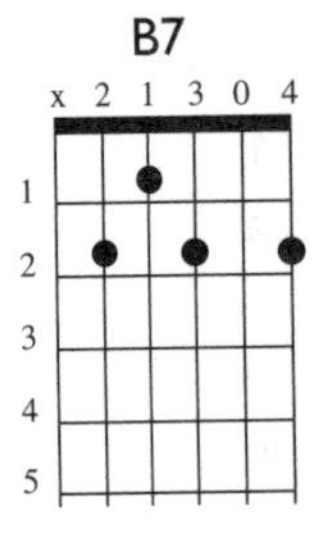

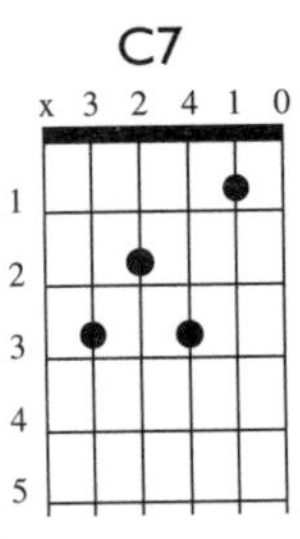

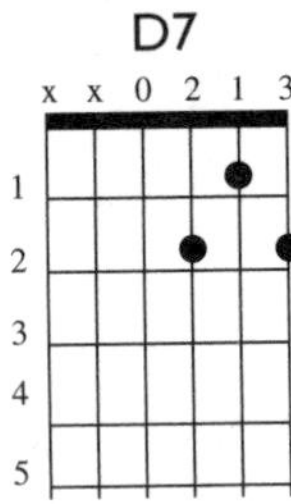

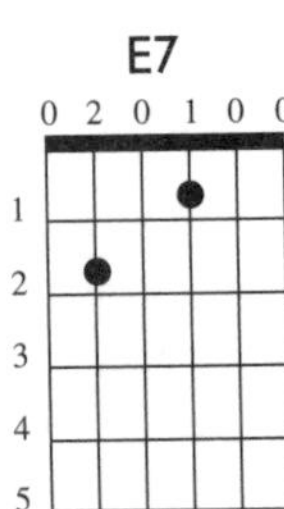

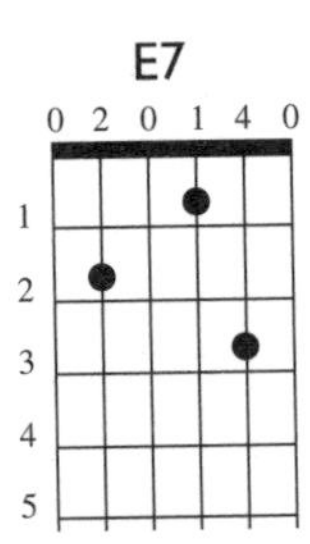

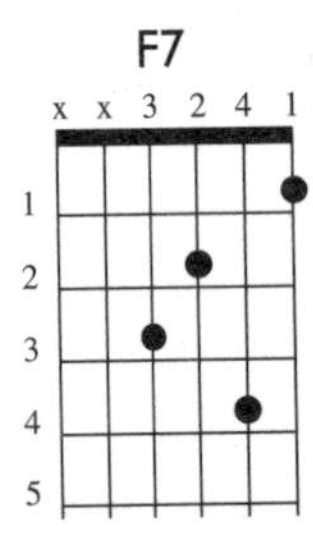

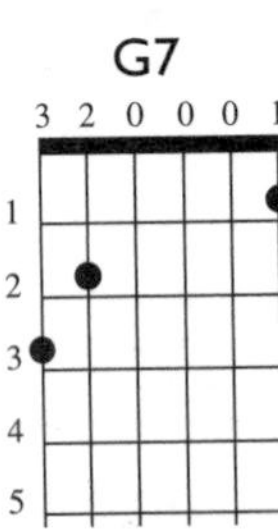


### Major and Minor Fingerings—Open or 1st position

These are not as common in the blues as dominant 7s, but are still important to master.

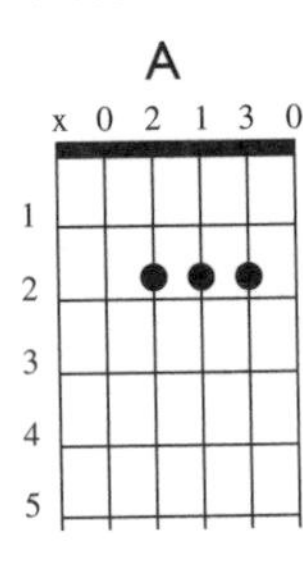

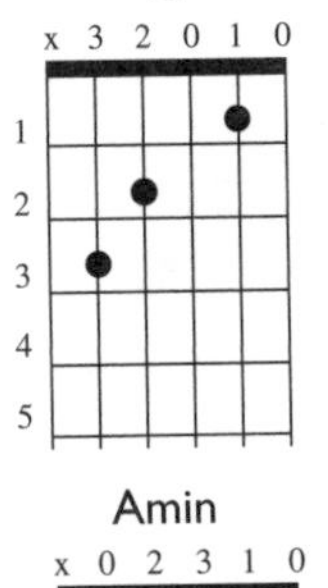

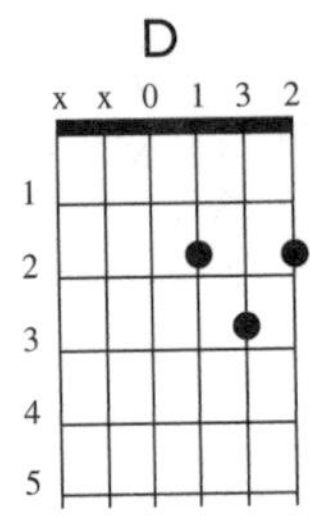

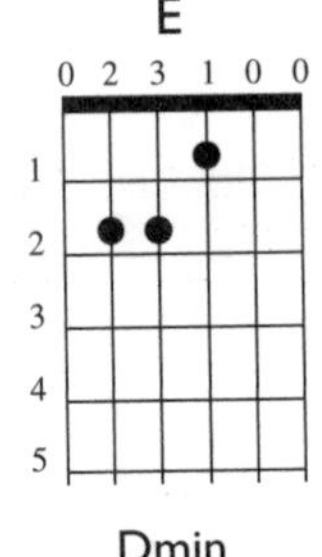

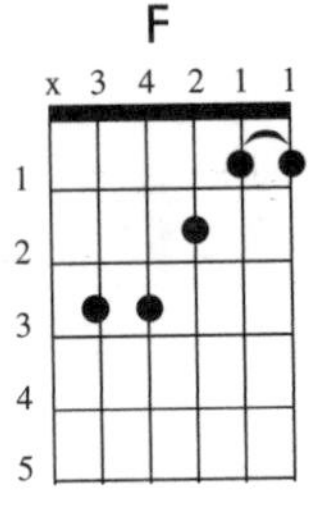

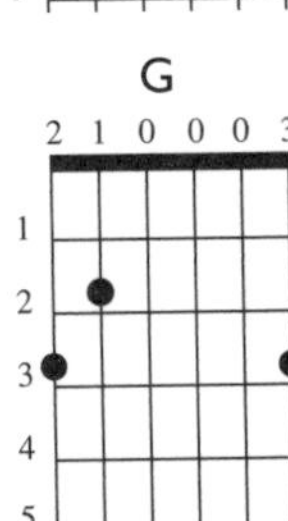

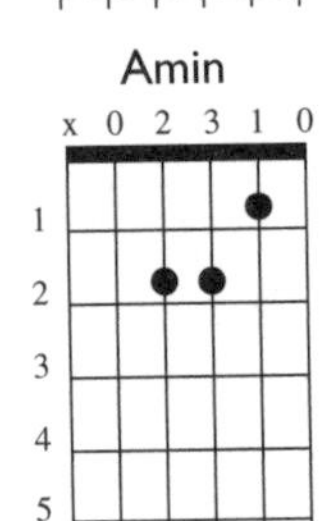

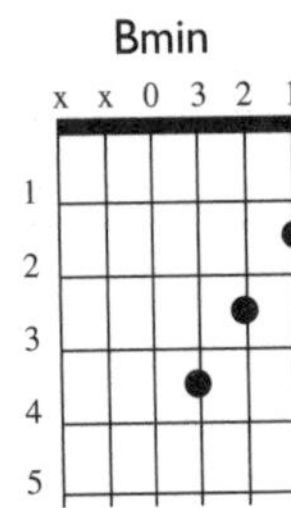

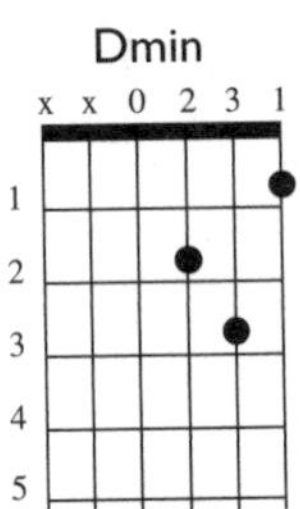

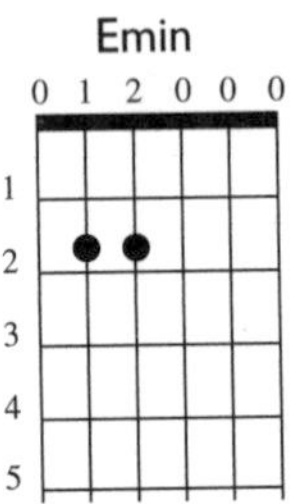


### Closed Voicings

These shapes are moveable. Slide them up or down the neck until you reach the root-note you need. The second dominant 7 shape has the same fingering as the C7 in open position, but here we need to mute the 1st string so we can play the chord on any fret. Be sure to mute the open strings in each of these voicings.

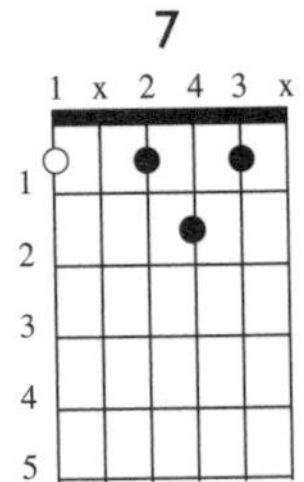

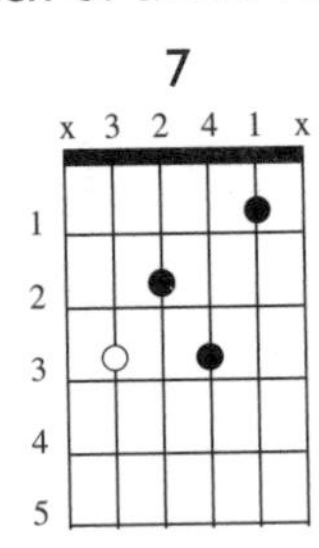

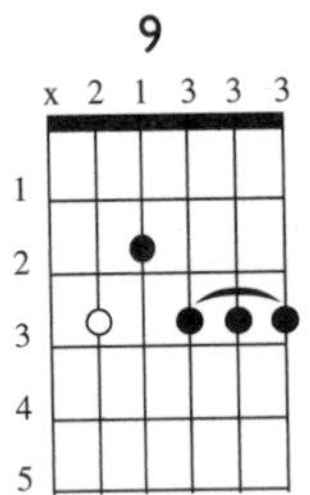

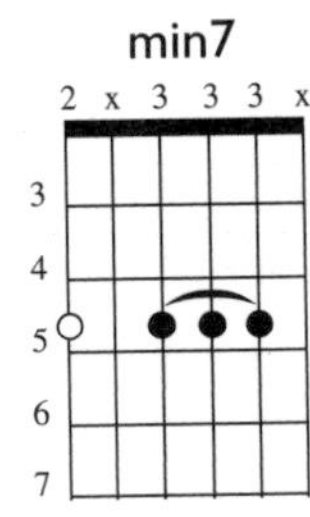


Maj7
1 x 3 4 2 x

# FINAL THOUGHTS

Congratulations on completing this book!

Hopefully, you are having a great time playing the acoustic blues. Now here is some advice to help you grow as a musician.

Play often, regularly and with passion. Learn everything between these covers. Every chapter is filled with techniques that all blues players need to know.

It may take awhile, but try to memorize everything in this book. Memorize the notes in every common scale and chord. This will increase your confidence and make the music a part of you.

Write out and practice each example in all the common keys. This will familiarize you with the fretboard and will prepare you for new musical situations. You'll be ready for anything.

Playing along with CDs will improve your musical ear. Figure out the key and the chords and play along with the band. If you can't figure out what the guitarist on the CD is doing, make up your own part. Improvise along with the CD. Also, try to figure out parts of the solos. If you can't get the exact notes, try to imitate the rhythms. This gets easier the more you do it.

Writing your own music is a real thrill. Take standard progressions and add new melodies and lyrics; or add new twists to tried-and-true patterns. Borrow ideas, but always try to add something new and original.

Learn to play with others. As soon as you can play a blues progression, stick your guitar neck out and say "let's jam." Music is a team sport. You'll learn faster and have a great time. Other players have been where you are, so they'll probably be patient with you. Play at open mics, parties, nursing homes, etc. Share your music. Applause is hard to beat; addictive, yet healthy for your soul.

Keep learning any way you can. A good teacher will help, as will other books and videos. Rob Fletcher's *Blues Grooves for Guitar* (National Guitar Workshop/Alfred #21895) will give you a complete look at blues rhythm guitar. Also, if you're interested in fingerstyle or country blues, check out my book, *Beginning Fingerstyle Guitar* (National Guitar Workshop/Alfred #14099).

The blues is a vocal music, so start singing. Most blues tunes are based on progressions in this book. Get the lyrics, open your mouth and let the music come out. You don't have to be Pavarotti to sing the blues. You just have to be yourself. So be yourself, play the blues and have fun.

If you have questions or comments about this book, you can write to loumanzi@snet.net.

IF YOU ENJOYED THIS BOOK, YOU'LL LOVE OUR SCHOOL
NATIONAL
GUITAR
WORKSHOP